Theology of Christian Marriage

Theology of
Christian Marriage

Walter Kasper

CROSSROAD · NEW YORK

1984

The Crossroad Publishing Company
370 Lexington Avenue
New York, N.Y. 10017

Published originally as *Zur Theologie der christlichen Ehe*
copyright © 1977 Matthias-Grünewald-Verlag, Mainz,
Federal Republic of Germany

Translated from the German by David Smith, English translation
copyright © 1980 Search Press Limited. All rights reserved.
No part of this book may be reproduced, stored in a retrieval system,
or transmitted, in any form or by any means, electronic, mechanical,
photocopying, recording, or otherwise, without the written permission of
The Crossroad Publishing Company.

Printed in the United States of America

Library of Congress Cataloging in Publication Data

Kasper, Walter.
  Theology of Christian marriage.

  Translation of: Zur Theologie der christlichen Ehe.
  Includes bibliographical references.
  1. Marriage—Moral and religious aspects—Catholic
Church. I. Title.
BX2250.K2713   1981   261.8'358   81-5444
ISBN 0-8245-0559-X

Contents

Introduction

There is no area of human life on which most people today are so dependent for personal happiness and fulfilment as that of love between man and woman, a love that is made lasting in marriage and family life. There is also no other sphere in which faith and life are so intimately in contact with each other as in marriage.

Marriage belongs to the order of creation and to the order of redemption. God created human beings as man and woman and the Bible tells us that this was good, even very good (see Gen. 1:27, 31). The bond that God wanted to establish between man and woman is an image or presentation of God's covenant with man that was definitively concluded in Jesus Christ and a likeness of God's love and faithfulness for man (see Eph. 5:21-33). Marriage between Christians, as a real aspect of God's creation, is also a real aspect of God's salvation.

It is very disturbing that there is hardly any other sphere

of human life today in which the discrepancy between the official teaching of the Church and the convictions and practice of very many Christians is so great as in questions of sexuality and marriage.[1] Many practicing Christians find the Church's teaching if not hostile to life, then at least very remote from life today. Precisely because the reality of creation and the reality of redemption are so closely interrelated in marriage, the radical changes that have taken place in recent years in man's understanding of himself and of the society he lives in and in the relationship between the sexes have had such a profound effect and have even led to a grave crisis. It is quite likely that the alienation of many Christians from the Church, or the merely partial identification of so many believers with their Church, may originate here.

In an attempt to minimize the problem, it has been suggested that all that is involved in this crisis is a number of questions of ethical behaviour, methods of family planning, or premarital sex. To be sure, these are all pressing problems, but they have to be seen in the context of the many radical changes that have been and still are taking place in our understanding of sexuality and of man as such. Individual moral norms can only be correctly understood and convincingly lived if Christian marriage is seen as a whole and in a new light. If they are not, they become letters that kill, are regarded as repressive, and finally are rejected.

Ethical questions will therefore be kept very much in the background in this book. [I shall be concerned instead to search for theological answers to such fundamental questions as: What is the real meaning of love and faithfulness in the Christian sense? What is the Christian understanding of

2 · Theology of Christian Marriage

marriage? On the basis of what understanding of faith can the life of man and woman together in marriage succeed in a meaningful and fulfilled human and Christian sense?]

It is not possible for a Christian theologian to answer these and similar questions simply on the basis of statements found in Scripture and tradition. This is because of the very close connection between the order of creation and the order of redemption in marriage. In any attempt to answer these questions, the teaching of Scripture and the Church's tradition must be related to what we know about marriage in the light of human experience in history and in the present.[2] In other words, the theology of marriage has to take seriously into account what the human sciences (medicine, psychology, sociology, cultural anthropology, ethnology and so on) have to say about marriage. This does not mean that the theology of marriage can be reduced to a number of anthropological statements, or that it should be adapted to the anonymous pressure of the modern social consciousness. Such an adaptation would certainly not further Christian freedom, which, in the imitation of Jesus, always calls for courage from Christians so that they can to some extent be nonconformists. This critical and liberating power can only be developed by Christian faith if in our understanding of marriage we allow a proper value to the right orientation of nature and grace (creation and redemption) and to the right distinction between them. For this reason, the first question that we have to consider here is that of human values in marriage. It is only against this background that the specifically Christian understanding of marriage can be reassessed.

The various reflections that follow are based on papers

that I have given at different times, on my work in connection with the synod of German bishops, and on my activities as an adviser and theologian on various commissions of the conference of German bishops. They have for the most part been adapted and rewritten for the present publication. I have included a great number of suggestions and have taken note of many critical observations in the final text. I have many people to thank, but above all my parents. I dedicate this book to my mother on her seventy-fifth birthday.

Chapter I

The Human Values of Marriage

1. THE TRADITIONAL DEFINITION OF MARRIAGE

Many different answers have been provided by various cultures and societies throughout the history of mankind to the question of the content and meaning of the shared life of man and woman in marriage.[3] Any examination of the results of modern research into the history of cultures reveals a confusing multiplicity in the reality of marriage. W. Schmidt's theory, that monogamy was the earliest historical form of marriage and that polygamy only emerged at a later stage and represents a decadent form, cannot be substantiated by historical evidence. The opposite thesis, which has been put forward forcibly by J. J. Bachofen, who believed that the reality commenced with a universal form of promiscuity, continued as polygamous and group marriage, and ended as monogamy, has been shown to be a construction based on liberal presuppositions. It would, however, be wrong to think of the modern understanding of marriage as a partnership as the norm, and to overlook the fact that married and family life have been regarded until only very recently in history in the context of the tribe, clan or extended family.

It is clear from the very many different ways in which marriage has been understood and practised in the history of human cultures that sexuality is and has always been characterized by a certain vagueness, openness and flexibility and that it has to be given form and definition by society. [It is striking that all the great movements of the modern era — liberalism, socialism and conservativism — have produced not only a political and economic theory of their own, but also a distinctive teaching about human sexuality and marriage.]

This inevitably leads us to ask whether the nature of marriage as such is in any sense permanent. Unlike Christian theologians during the late baroque and the neoscholastic periods, Thomas Aquinas was concerned with this question, and his teaching about the natural law has become classical.[4] His answer to the question as to whether marriage is natural was that there is a natural inclination in man to marry, but that marriage takes place in actuality through an act of human freedom.[5] Man's nature has been given both to him and to his freedom. With regard to marriage, Thomas maintained that human nature was not unchangeable.[6] This made it quite easy for him to accept the multiplicity of concrete forms in which marriage had expressed itself at various stages of human history.[7] Thomas's conclusion is that marriage can only exist in historical forms and that it is the nature of marriage to be historical.

The task of the Christian revelation in history is, according to Thomas, to help people who are inclined to error and weakened by sin, to know the meaning of human nature at a deeper level, and to make it a practical reality.[8] The Christian reality of marriage is therefore a historical reality, although the fulness of time was attained in Jesus Christ according to faith. The Christian understanding of marriage therefore has an ultimate and universal validity. This universality means, however, that it is not possible to make any one particular historical or cultural reality of marriage absolute. Christianity has rather to remain open to all cultures and to all historical change. It is therefore hardly surprising that the Catholic history of teaching about marriage and the Catholic law of marriage have been subject to considerable change.[9] The Catholic ethos of marriage has often only been able to make headway in the face of difficulties in opposition to dualistic and Manichaean tendencies. Sexuality and marriage have frequently been devalued in the history of Christianity. This is beyond dispute, as is the fact that, in the course of history, the Christian and human dignity of marriage has again and again been defended against many dangerous tendencies. In this historical process, the Christian understanding of marriage has become "the womb of our western culture and its spiritual attitudes."[10]

Thomas Aquinas wrote his great theological synthesis in an attempt to express in an all-embracing form a classical Christian view of all human values, including those of marriage. His aim was to integrate marriage into a total Christian understanding of humanity and the world. He did this by going back to Augustine's doctrine of the three goods or values (*bona*) of marriage: descendants, mutual love and faithfulness, and the sacramental sign.[11] Whereas Augustine was concerned principally with the grounds for marriage, however, Thomas was able to use those grounds to express the human dignity of marriage. Purely sensual love tended, he believed, to break away from humanity's total orientation in life, assume an independent value of its own and thus threaten the dignity of human beings. It was, however, integrated into the total meaning of human life by the three goods of marriage. Human sexuality was placed at the service of mankind within marriage by the begetting of descendants. Sexuality was incorporated into personal love and self-surrender by the mutual love and faithfulness of the two spouses; this also provided a guarantee that a woman was valued not simply as a sexual being, but as a partner. Human faithfulness became a sign of God's faithfulness to the covenant in Jesus Christ and was incorporated into humanity's orientation towards God as the ultimate ground and objective of its existence by the sacramental sign of marriage.

This, then, is the impressive teaching of the Christian tradition, as summarized by Thomas Aquinas. It had a very deep influence on our western culture. It stood or fell, however, with the total Christian understanding of humanity and the world as such, and the process of secularization that has been taking place in recent centuries has inevitably led to the breaking up of this synthesis and a crisis in the traditional Christian understanding of marriage. We have therefore to undertake once again the task that Thomas

Aquinas so successfully performed in the high Middle Ages, but we are bound to do so under new presuppositions.

2. THE CHANGE IN OUR UNDERSTANDING OF MARRIAGE: AN OPPORTUNITY AND A CRISIS

The present crisis in marriage can be traced back to a number of historical causes, which cannot unfortunately be discussed in detail here.[12] One of the reasons, however, can be indicated. The crisis must be seen against the background of the transition from an earlier agrarian society to a modern industrialized and urbanized civilization. One of the most striking characteristics of the new society that is emerging as a result of this process is the division between the private and the public sphere. In the past, marriage was not simply a private and personal community existing within the framework of a nuclear family based on partnership. It was also an economic and producing community within the framework of the extended family. In modern technological society, a division has occurred between the sphere of marriage and the family on the one hand and that of work and professional life on the other. This has led, especially in the many cases where a wife is professionally employed, to an extensive collapse of the economic function of marriage and the family, their loss of function with regard to social welfare and care, and their reduction to or concentration on personal relationships with the emphasis on sympathy and love.

The discovery of the problem of overpopulation (Malthus) and the evolution of new forms of family planning and birth control have furthered the emancipation of marriage and family life. Marriage is now much less dependent on social determinants. It can also, at least in principle, be separated from natural conditions of reproduction and procreation, as a result of the new scientific insights that have been gained in the past century or so. [Perhaps the most important discovery for the improved position of woman and our understanding of marriage as a partnership is that made in 1875, when it was learnt that new life arose from the fusion of one sperm-cell and one egg-cell and that the woman consequently made an active and not simply a receptive contribution to the process of procreation.]

The opportunity that is provided by this change in marriage and family life is that marriage may perhaps be made more deeply personalized. Even now, the personal and intimate sphere of that way of life is experienced by countless people as a "reservoir of opposition to the increasing emptiness of the world."[13] It is clear that marriage and family life are the necessary anthropological corrective to a growing rationalization and even brutalization of public life. Individuals find that they have become increasingly lonely in an increasingly anonymous world, and for them marriage is a refuge in their search for security. This is one very important reason why the institution of marriage has shown an astonishing stability despite all the questionings and threats to which it has been subjected. Certainly the relationship of mutual partnership between man and wife in modern marriage deserves to be helped, supported and promoted in every way by the Church.

In addition to this positive opportunity for deeper personalization, there is also, however, a danger that this personal relationship in marriage that has been to a great extent set free from social and biological conditioning may be restricted to the exclusively private sphere, and therefore may be without any moral obligations to society as a whole. Now that love has lost its element of risk because of the pill, it is in constant danger of also losing both its importance and its gravity. Since the Romantic period, people's understanding of freedom and marriage has become more and more individualized and privatized, and this has in turn led to a deeper questioning of marriage as an institution.

During the first half of the present century, there was a great deal of discussion about free love, experimental marriage and companionate marriage. Nowadays, there is a marked tendency toward emancipation from the compulsions associated with earlier forms of marriage based on a distinctive synthesis of ideas drawn from neo-Marxism and psychoanalysis. The so-called sexual revolution is directed, on the one hand, toward liberation from the institutionalization that society has imposed on human sexuality and, on the other, towards dissociation from nature and the limitations imposed by it (fertility and procreation).

Even more dangerous than this tendency, however, is the fact that the more fully it is limited to the purely private sphere, the more marriage is exposed to and unprotected from influences exerted by the current norms of society and public life. The values of twentieth-century society, which is based on performance, production and consumption and prestige, are always threatening to penetrate into the sphere of marriage and family life. Human sexuality, in other words, is in constant danger of becoming merely sex, a commodity for consumption, pleasure, or exploitation. The privatization of marriage, then, does not necessarily lead to its personalization. It frequently results in marriage becoming a totally depersonalized thing.

These opportunities and dangers involved in the contemporary reality of marriage present the Church with a challenge to which it is bound to respond in its preaching and practice. The fundamental question is whether the positive possibilities of this new understanding of marriage as a personal partnership will be successfully exploited and the objective structures within which marriage has hitherto existed in the tradition of the Church can be adapted. It is this question concerning the relationship between the personal and the objective or institutional aspects of marriage that has formed the constant background to the two great debates on marriage that have taken place in recent years in the Church: the controversy about birth regulation and the discussion about the indissolubility of marriage. Both these problems should, of course, be seen against the background of the transition that is occurring at present from a static and natural understanding of reality to a more dynamic, personal and historical understanding.

One question that arises in this context is whether it is possible for such a development to take place without breaking radically with the tradition of the Church. It would be true to say that the traditional Catholic teaching about marriage has been dominated by an objective and institutional understanding. The definiton of the consent to marriage provided by canon law is very interesting in this respect. It is defined as an act of the will in which each party gives and receives the exclusive and lasting right to the body in respect of the acts appropriate to the begetting of descendants.[14]

Fortunately, the draft of the new canon law on marriage is very different and every effort has been made in it to overcome this narrow and objective view of marriage that is nowadays almost incomprehensible. The earlier tradition in the Church shows evidence of a much wider and more all-embracing view of marriage. According to the Roman Catechism of 1566, for example, the primary reason for marriage is the community of man and woman for the purpose of mutual help so that together they will more easily be able to bear the difficulties of life and especially those of old age.[15] This idea was taken up again in the encyclical *Casti Conubii* of 1930, where it was called the further definition of marriage.[16]

The final breakthrough came with the pastoral constitution *Gaudium et Spes* of the Second Vatican Council (1965), in which marriage is defined as a personal community within which the partners give and accept each other.[17] The objective and institutional aspects of marriage were obviously understood in a new way in this conciliar document and made subordinate to the more personal view. This process was continued in the encyclical *Humanae Vitae* (1968). In the first part of this letter, marriage is seen in what is, for a church document, a surprisingly new light, that is, as a personal community.[18] On the other hand, however, many of the statements made in the second part, which deals with the permitted methods of birth regulation, give the impression of a distinct return to an earlier natural and biological view of marriage. It was, of course, this part of the encyclical that occasioned such criticism.

Although the Church has so far not succeeded in satisfactorily reintegrating the different aspects of marriage within a personal perspective, a beginning has certainly been made. It is at least already clear in which direction theologians ought to be thinking with regard to marriage.[19] It is not so much a question of personalizing marriage to the extent of stripping it of all its essential institutional elements or freeing it from its existing structures. It is rather a question of preserving, as in the past, the inner unity of the three traditional values emphasized by Augustine and Thomas Aquinas; in other words, of continuing to envisage marriage in its natural, social, personal and sacramental aspects, but of no longer taking the begetting of descendants as the only basis for marriage. [The point of departure for Christian thinking about marriage today should be the aspect of mutual love and faithfulness.] The essential aspect of the person in marriage should, in other words, be determined not naturally, but relationally. If we are successful in developing such a view of marriage, it will be possible to testify to the reality of the fundamental principle stated by the Second Vatican Council: "The beginning, the subject and the goal of all social institutions is and must be the human person, which for its part and by its very nature stands completely in need of social life."[20]

It is, of course, inevitable that a renewed vision of marriage of this kind will lead to concrete questions and practical consequences. In this whole process of rethinking, however, we should not simply be conscious of the breaking down of old forms. We should also recognize the opportunity provided for a deeper personal understanding of the reality of marriage.

3. APPROACHES TO A NEW UNDERSTANDING OF MARRIAGE

(i) Personal love

If, in defining the essential aspect of love, we speak of the mutual love of the partners, we are, of course, not using the word "love" in a superficial or sentimental way.[21] If we think of love at a deeper level, that is, in the sense in which we understand it here, it can be seen as the most fundamental of all realities. Finite being is dependent on and in constant need of fulfilment by another reality. A person, as a finite being with such a need, is also always striving for fulfilment by material, biological, and spiritual goods. None of these, however, is able to satisfy him or her completely. A man or woman needs a partner who is in accordance with himself or herself (see Gen. 2:20ff). Human persons have dignity because they exist for their own sakes. A person therefore only finds fulfilment when he or she is accepted as a person. Human fulfilment therefore only exists in personal love, that is, in a love that says: I want you to be; it is good that you are. This love consents to the other as the other. An essential aspect of the dialectics of love is that it joins two persons together in the most intimate way and by doing so at the same time sets them free to independent personal existence.

People only exist in their bodies and in their relationship with the world. Sexuality is also determined by this. It is not a partial determination, but a fundamental and total datum, by which a person is deeply and completely marked even in the most sublime spiritual aspects of being and doing.[22] On the other hand, human sexuality is also personally determined and has the task of expressing and mediating intersubjective communication. It is only to the extent that it is integrated into personal bonds that human sexuality can be realized in the human sense. If these personal bonds are lacking, human sexuality can only result in the disintegration and loss of dignity of the human person. The most all-embracing form of personal bond between man and woman is marriage. More than any other form of human relationship, marriage embraces the whole person of both partners in all their dimensions. The full community of sexual relationships or sexual intercourse obviously has a meaningful place in marriage, because it is only there that it is contained within an all-embracing human community involving the whole of the partners' life and fate.

The corporeal nature of the human person and of the community of marriage as such means, however, that it is never possible to speak purely personally of marriage. It is obvious from everyday experience that at least a minimum of physical (health), social and economic requirements are needed if a marriage is to be successful. To express this in a more abstract way, we may say that love includes justice—the justice that gives to the other his or her due and thus restores an equality in the relationship between the external matter and the person.[23] The love that accepts and consents to the other as the other also gives to the other his or her due. Without this justice, it would be dishonest and empty. An all-embracing personal view of marriage also includes both objective and institutional elements. A renewed theology of marriage must therefore be on its guard not only against a one-sided objectivization and a tendency to overemphasize the institutional aspect of the reality, but also against a too individualistic and romantic or idealistic understanding of the part played by the person in marriage. Marriage, in other words, should not be seen purely as a love relationship. It must also be seen within the framework of the actual social and economic conditions of human freedom.

The Church clearly has an important ministry in the sphere of marriage. It has the task of helping and counselling individuals. It must also use its influence politically and take active steps legally within the revision of canon law to ensure as far as possible the success of marriages in their early and their later stages. Perhaps the most important service that the Church has to carry out, however, is that of making young people capable of loving on the basis of Christian faith. The fundamental law of any life led in faith is "He who loses his life will find it" (see Matt. 10:39 etc.). An increase of faith is therefore the most important preparation for marriage that any Christian can undertake.

(ii) Fruitful love

One of the essential aspects of love is that it does not stay with itself, but tends to be fruitful. This essential connection between married love and fruitfulness was, in the past, usually given a purely biological justification.[24] This, however, proved to be quite an unsatisfactory explanation because, in contrast to the sexuality of animals, human sexuality displayed certain distinctive features which showed that its function was not restricted to the preservation of the species. One way in which human sexuality differs quite radically from that of animals is that there is in man no seasonal rhythm of sexual impulse (a rutting season or season in heat). Man's sexual urge is constantly active and this results in a surfeit of sexual impulse that is in need of normalization and cultivation. When we speak of the need to humanize sexuality, we do not mean repression or inhibition. Human culture is based to a great extent on sexual asceticism, and the sublimation of sexual urges has led to the advance of civilization.[25] One of the aspects of the cultivation of human sexuality is the expression of personal love in marriage. It is through this application of sexuality that the partners are able to experience mutual happiness. In the past, eros or sexual desire was frequently defamed and there is an urgent need to correct this tendency where it still persists. It is clear that human sexuality cannot be restricted simply to the sex act and the reproduction of the species. The fruitfulness of marriage can therefore not be justified purely on the basis of biology.

The fruitfulness of marriage comes from the inner essence of personal love itself.[26] If it is essential for love to empty itself, it must therefore be impossible for true love to stay with itself. It is inevitably impelled to realization, objectivization and embodiment in a shared third party. As the fruit of shared love, a child is not simply an external and fortuitous addition to the mutual love of the partners in marriage; it is rather the realization and fulfilment of that love. This does not mean, of course, that a marriage which is childless for reasons that cannot be justified by the two partners is bound to be unfulfilled and unhappy. Love has a value and a meaning of its own. It does, however, become a perversion of itself when it becomes deliberately and selfishly closed in on itself and consciously excludes fruitfulness for purely egoistic reasons. When this happens, it eventually loses contact with its central being and reality. The two partners normally find themselves in a new way in their child or children, and the latter can only thrive as human beings if they are secure in the mutual love of the parents. Although a distinction is usually made between descendants and mutual love as the first and second purpose of marriage, these two aspects really form a single organic whole. Even if the immediate reason for the physical union of the partners is not to beget further descendants, but to deepen and enrich their own experience of mutual love, this is of indirect benefit to the descendants who are already in the family (*bonum prolis*). This physical union is in contradiction to the meaning of love and therefore immoral if it is selfishly closed in on itself and not open to the greater reality of "we."

When it transcends itself in children, love at the same time takes its place in the wider context of human society as a whole. By begetting and bringing up children, the partners in marriage are contributing to the continued existence of society and ensuring the survival of mankind in the future. This is not simply an increase in or an addition to the number of human beings in society. It is an authentic process of procreation and education, in which human culture is mediated and history is transmitted. This inner connection between the commandment to man to be fruitful and his cultural task is stressed in the Old Testament: "Be fruitful and multiply and fill the earth and subdue it" (Gen.1:28). It is clear from this that the fruitfulness of marriage is not based on human biological nature, but on humanity's cultural, social and historical task. Marriage and the family, then, cannot be regarded by Christians as a purely private matter. They are public and, in the widest sense of the word, political.[27]

It should therefore be clear by now that human fruit-fulness can never be exclusively dependent on a biological or natural rhythm. It must above all be subordinated to man's sense of moral responsibility. Responsible parenthood is in no way autocratic or arbitrary. The human person, with a personal conscience, is always placed within previously given relationships. Four criteria on which a moral decision can be based emerge as a result of what we have said so far. Firstly, there must be respect for the dignity of the other partner in marriage and responsibility for the continuation and deepening of mutual love. Secondly, there must be respon-sibility for the children already present in the family and still to come. Thirdly, there must also be responsibility for the future of society and mankind as a whole. Fourthly, there must be respect for the inner meaning of human nature as created by God and given to humans, not for unlimited ex-ploitation and manipulation, but so that they can achieve their cultural and social task. It would be an act of ultimate cynicism to strive for a freedom that is liberated from all natural bonds. Such an act would also lead to agnostic divi-sion between spirit and matter. This would be in direct op-position to the Christian theory and practice of consent to the world and the body.

These four criteria should not lead us into the sphere of detailed casuistry. They provide us rather with a broad outline of the form and meaning of fruitfulness in marriage. They represent a concrete model which is, in the sense of the classical Aristotelian and Thomist doctrine of the natural law, not abstract and deductive, but historical and based on man's experience and normal behaviour and manners in society in whatever period he is living. It is by considering these criteria that a Christian can make conscientious personal decisions, about life and marriage within the framework of the community of believers and the Church's teaching. They should inspire people to live their married and family life in a fully responsible, human and Christian way.

(iii) Faithfulness in love

[The shared responsibility of the partners for their children is one of the most convincing arguments in favour of the indissolubility of marriage.] This third good of marriage, faithfulness, can, however, be more directly attributed to the essential meaning of love itself. Unlike an animal, a human being lacks the security of instinctive behaviour in a clearly defined and specific environment. As anthropologists say, one is open to the world.[28] If one is to avoid losing oneself in this openness, with its surfeit of stimuli, one has to give himself, in free responsibility, his or her own outline, face, and form. This openness and lack of fulfilment is the other side of one's freedom. It is, however, freedom that enables human beings to give themselves a definitive form.[29] In this respect, freedom is the opposite of arbitrary choice, which acts in the name of freedom, but believes that it is possible always to begin at the beginning and again and again to cancel every decision in which people realize themselves. This arbitrary and dissipated bachelor form of freedom is perhaps the greatest threat to true freedom, since, if nothing is definitive and everything can be changed again and again, everything assumes an equal importance or lack of importance and nothing is taken seriously. It is only when there are really irreversible decisions that life becomes a real risk and a genuine adventure. True freedom is therefore realized in faithfulness.

Freedom that realizes itself in faithfulness is best expressed in the form of dialogue. It is for this reason that Nietzsche called a human being an animal that can promise.[30] This promise tends inwardly towards definitiveness. According to Gabriel Marcel, loving another person means telling him or her: You will not die.[31] The bond of faithfulness in marriage is essentially not a yoke imposed on the two partners, depriving them of their freedom. On the contrary, it is the most sublime way in which their freedom is realized, an existential expression of no longer being able to act differently. The marital bond in freedom makes the partners free in a new way. Above all, it makes them free from the moods and fickleness of the moment. In this way, faithfulness is a victory over time.

[Man and woman are able to find their definitive status in this faithfulness. They become "one flesh" or "one" (Gen. 2:24; Mark 10:8; Eph. 5:31); in other words, they become a "we" person. The marital bond of faithfulness creates something that transcends the single person and binds the history of two people definitively and at the deepest level together.]

What do we mean, then, by the bond of marriage? To define it negatively, it is not a kind of metaphysical hypostasis existing above or alongside the personal love of the partners (the "objectivist" view). Nor is it simply a factor that becomes absorbed into each act of love, with the result that, if these acts cease, as they do when there is a prolonged period of unfaithfulness, the marriage is *de facto* at an end (this is the "actualist" view; see below, Chapter III). A promise of faithfulness made in freedom is permanently inscribed in the history of the two persons. It is an intersubjective ontological intention and determination made in freedom through which a man and a woman reach their definitive status in and through their bond of unity.

Whenever a person commits himself or herself totally and definitively in this way to the ground and objective of his existence, then, according to Christian faith, God inevitably enters the arena.[32] The definitive bond of faithfulness in marriage has, in other words, an essential religious dimension. In this bond, a person commits himself or herself to an existence, the end of which cannot be foreseen, and which is something that is unconditioned and cannot be called into question. One touches the ultimate mystery of his or her existence; this mystery concerns one deeply and yet remains hidden. People commit themselves, in other words, to something that they do not possess and that they will never fully possess. They live on hope and trust and neither spouse can ever fully account for this. They enjoy themselves, so to speak, at somebody else's expense. Marital faithfulness, then, is both a symbol that points to a reality beyond itself and a participation in the faithfulness of God. In this definitive and unconditioned way, two people can accept each other only because they have already been definitively and unconditionally accepted. Faithfulness in marriage is therefore a place where transcendence can possibly be experienced.

None of these statements can, it is true, be made purely objective. The phenomena to which they point can be interpreted in many different ways and are ultimately dependent on a definitive interpretation. It is, however, not simply a matter of pure chance that, in all human cultures, marriage is contracted under religious symbols. The Catholic Church describes marriage as a sacrament and this interpretation of the reality of marriage has not simply been imposed from outside.[33] Even in its universally human form, marriage already has an orientation towards this interpretation and fulfilment. Human faithfulness is, as it were, the grammar by means of which God's faithfulness, definitively revealed in Jesus Christ, can be spelt out. Just as a poem cannot be derived from the rules of grammar, so too can the sacramental reality of marriage not be traced back to a purely anthropological origin. The sacramentality of marriage is rather an irreducibly new, creative concentration and determination of the reality that is already implied universally and in an undetermined way in the human form of marriage. The sacrament of marriage fulfils in an irreducible way what has so far been suggested phenomenologically as the essential being of marriage.

Chapter II

The Sacramental Dignity of Marriage

1. ITS FOUNDATION IN THE HISTORY OF SALVATION: THE UNITY OF CREATION AND REDEMPTION

(i) Its basis in creation

The attitude of the Old Testament authors towards human sexuality, love between man and woman, and marriage and the begetting of children, is extremely open, frank, and positive. The Song of Solomon, for example, is a celebration of human love, which is presented as an experience of great happiness and fulfilment. The experience is certainly not seen in terms of naive sexual euphoria. The biblical authors were certainly also aware of the other aspects of human sexuality—its temptations and brokenness, the pain of giving birth, the oppression of woman by man, unfaithfulness and guilt. But sexuality is never fundamentally devalued or defamed in the Old Testament. The sexual difference between man and woman and their sexual encounter with each other are presented as belonging to the order of creation and as part of God's plan. Of God's creation it is said that "it was very good" (Gen. 1:31), and this also applies to the relationship between man and woman.

This relationship is so fundamental in the Bible that it forms part of the theological definition of humanity's being that is provided in Genesis, when people are described as having been made in God's image: "So God created man in his own image . . . male and female he created them" (Gen. 1:27).[34] The sexual difference clearly forms an essential part of humanity's created being. Humanity as such does not exist. It exists only as man and woman. It is only in togetherness that human existence can be fulfilled in the fully human sense. (This mystery between man and woman is so deep that the covenant between man and woman is, in the Bible, the image and likeness of God's covenant with man and the reproduction of his love, faithfulness and creative power. (In this way, an almost inestimable value is given to marriage, and hostility between the sexes is excluded from the relationship.

Despite the fact that the Bible raises human sexuality and the relationship between man and woman to such a high level, it never deifies sex or erotic love in the way that it was deified in the other religions of the ancient Near East. On the contrary, this sacralization and deification of sexuality was regarded by the biblical authors as typically pagan and was therefore rejected by them. This desacralization is based on the Old Testament faith in creation and the consequent distinction made between the creator and the creature. It is only if people have this natural or rather creaturely view of sexuality that they can be inwardly free and responsible for themselves in this sphere as in others. As factors in human creation, sexuality and marriage never have an ultimate value. They can only have a penultimate value because, in their created goodness and beauty, they point to something beyond themselves. Like other aspects of creation, they do not have their basis or their aim in themselves. For this reason, people cannot find ultimate fulfilment in a purely horizontal love relationship. The finite and limited love between man and woman is rather the image of an unconditioned and definitive acceptance of man that can only come from God. Both in its greatness and in its limitations, then, marriage is an actual form of human hope of salvation. It is therefore possible to speak, in this sense, of a natural sacrament of marriage, as indeed the Church's tradition does.

(ii) Instituted by Jesus Christ?

In the Old Testament, the covenant between man and woman becomes the "image and likeness" of the covenant between God and man (see, for example, Hos. 1,3; Jer. 2,3, 31; Ezek. 16,23; Isa. 54,62). Marriage, then, is the grammar that God uses to express his love and faithfulness. This covenant between God and humanity is realized in a definitive and unsurpassable way in Jesus Christ, who is in person God's covenant with human beings. He is the bridegroom of God's people of the new covenant (see Mark 2:19). It is through him that we are definitively invited to share the wedding feast in the kingdom of God (see Matt. 22:2ff). Our understanding of marriage as a sacrament is based above all on this understanding of marriage as a sign of God's covenant.[35] The sacramental nature of marriage cannot be proved by using individual words of institution. It is more important to show that marriage is sacramental because it is fundamentally related to the saving work of Jesus Christ.

Jesus' attitude towards marriage[36] is expressed most clearly in Mark 10:2-9. In a controversy with the pharisees, Jesus is here confronted with the question as to whether it is lawful for a man to release his wife. The controversy as a whole is about the interpretation of Deuteronomy 24:1, which is disputed by the Jews. Jesus does not become involved in the casuistry of the controversy, but raises the whole matter to a higher level and points to the original order of God's creation. His conclusion is that "what God has joined together, let no man put asunder."

If this statement is viewed simply from the outside, it points to a strengthening on Jesus' part of the law. If, however, we consider it within the whole context of Jesus' preaching and teaching, it is clear that the level of the law as such is completely transcended. Like the prophets, Jesus was aware of human hardness of heart. It is only when God gives people a "new heart" (see Jer. 31:33) that they are capable of living in accordance with God's will. This messianic expectation was fulfilled in Jesus' proclamation of the closeness of the eschatological kingdom of God. It would therefore be wrong to understand his pronouncement about marriage as a legal statement. It is above all a prophetic and messianic statement, an affirmation of salvation and grace. [In Jesus' proclamation, then, marriage is seen both as part of the original order of creation and as an aspect of the order of salvation of God in his kingdom of love and faithfulness.]

The coming of the kingdom of God is closely linked to the

coming of Jesus. He is the new Moses who, with his full authority, goes back beyond the words of Moses and surpasses them eschatologically. He is the coming of the kingdom of God in person. This aspect of his appearance was developed in the early communities of the Church after the Easter event, and the Christological link with marriage was also expressed at a relatively early period in the history of Christianity. There is a reference to this in the first letter to the Corinthians, where Paul says that Christians should marry "in the Lord" (1 Cor. 7:39). It is clear from this and other references that marriage is included in humanity's new being in Christ that is based on baptism. This is why marriage and family life feature again and again in the household codes of the New Testament as a place where Christian faith proves its value in a very special way. In practice, the partners in Christian marriage behave in such a way towards each other that their conduct is always oriented towards the obedience, love, faithfulness and self-giving of Christ for his Church. In this sense, marriage is a Christian emergency because it is in it that "being of the mind of Christ" (Phil. 2:5) in obedience, love and faithfulness is made a reality here and now in a very special way (see, for example, Col. 3:18 ff; 1 Pet. 3:1-7; 1 Tim. 2:8-15; Titus 2:1-6).

The most important of these household codes for our purpose is found in Ephesians 5:21-33.[37] In this text, the covenant between man and wife in marriage is seen as the image of the covenant between Christ and the Church. The passage closes with the words: "This is a great mystery (mysterion) and I take it to mean Christ and the Church." A sacramental interpretation of this passage was suggested in the later tradition of the Church by the translation in the Vulgate of the Greek concept of *mysterion* by the Latin word *sacramentum*. Most scholars are agreed now, however, that the later idea of sacrament should not be presupposed in this biblical pericope. Three different interpretations have been suggested in recent years and these can be summarized as follows. The word *mysterion* can be understood as the hidden meaning of the passage quoted (Gen. 2:24). It can be seen as referring to marriage itself. Thirdly, it can be regarded as pointing to the connection between Christ and his Church. It is certainly this last interpretation that is most fully in accordance with the linguistic usage of the Pauline and the Deutero-Pauline letters, since, in those writings, *mysterion* always points to God's eternal plan of salvation and his saving will that became a historical reality in Jesus Christ and a present reality in the Church. It is within this all-embracing reality of salvation that marriage is included.

Marriage, then, is in its own way a form by means of which God's eternal love and faithfulness, revealed in Jesus Christ, are made historically present. The love and faithfulness existing between Christ and his Church is therefore not simply an image or example of marriage, nor is the self-giving of man and wife in marriage an image and likeness of Christ's giving of himself to the Church. The love that exists between man and wife is rather a sign that makes the reality present, in other words, an epiphany of the love and faithfulness of God that was given once and for all time in Jesus Christ and is made present in the Church. In this sense, it is possible to see that the sacramental nature of marriage is indicated in Ephesians 5:32, as did the Council of Trent.[38]

It is, however, hardly possible to base the sacramentality of marriage exclusively on a few isolated passages in Scripture. It is only possible to do this by applying the argument of convergence. The sacramentality of marriage emerges from Ephesians 5:21ff above all on the basis of a number of suppositions. These are "that the total self-giving of the person that takes place in marriage implies a relationship with God as the ground and the aim of this self-giving; that Christ included marriage in the Christian order; that the relationship involved in marriage is different from other relationships between human beings; that, wherever fundamental signs that are intimately connected with the life of Christians and the Church exist and these point to the reality of grace, such signs cannot, within the new covenant, be empty and meaningless; that every community of Christians in Christ includes a making present of Christ and therefore of the Church (see Matt. 18:20), with the result that this can also be said especially of the smallest community in Christ, namely marriage. It is possible to understand the sacramental nature of marriage and its historical institution on the basis of these presuppositions. [Christ instituted the sacrament by establishing the new covenant as an eternal sign of God's grace and by giving that sign a sacramental reality. This sacramental sign represents and expresses the unity of Christ and the Church."[39]]

(iii) The development of marriage as a sacrament in the tradition of the Church

It was not until relatively late in the history of the Church that marriage was declared to be a sacrament. From that time, that is the twelfth century, onwards, explicit statements were made by the Church's teaching office.[40] We cannot, of course, enter into details here about this complicated historical process. It should, however, be clear that the fact that marriage was not until that time explicitly regarded as a sacrament did not mean that it was on the contrary seen, until about the twelfth century, simply as a secular reality and only later sacralized. The very opposite is true. The whole of reality, including marriage, was regarded almost without question as sacral, and it was only as a result of the long and difficult controversies that took place in the eleventh and twelfth centuries, following the Gregorian reform of the Church, that the latter became free from involvement in the dynastic structure and political order of the Carolingian and Ottonian empire and its overemphasis of the sacral nature of reality. It was at this time that the process of secularization first began, and it was only after this secular view of reality had become firmly established that individual signs and rites could be consciously presented as sacraments. The conscious appreciation of marriage as a sacrament, then, presupposes its desacralization and its recognition as a reality of creation. This also applies to marriage in a very special sense. In each sacrament, after all, an element of the world (water, bread, wine, for example) becomes an effective sign of salvation. Whereas birth, however, is not baptism, marriage as such is really a making present of God's love and faithfulness in Jesus Christ for a baptized Christian. Among baptized Christians, then, marriage as a reality of creation is at once and at the same time a sacrament of Christ.

This close connection between the order of creation and the order of redemption in Christian marriage is of importance in our assessment of the controversy between Catholicism and Protestantism about the sacramental nature of marriage.[41] Luther called marriage a "worldly affair"[42] and an "external and worldly thing."[43] He did not, however, mean by these statements that marriage was a purely profane reality, since, only a few lines further on, he called marriage "God's work and commandment," a holy state worthy of God's blessing.[44] He was only concerned to stress the fact that marriage was part, not of the order of salvation, but of the order of creation.[45] The controversy about the sacramentality of marriage, then, was not a dispute about an isolated statement about faith, but a far-reaching debate about the fundamental problem of the relationship between the order of creation and the order of redemption and the relationship between the Church and the world. The whole Catholic-Protestant controversy, which was fundamentally about human justification by God, was concentrated here in one concrete and individual question, that of the sacramentality of marriage. This question is of great contemporary importance because the increasing numbers of marriages between Catholics and Protestants today make it necessary for us to strive towards a greater degree of agreement about this central point of controversy and eventually to find a solution to the problem of the sacramentality of marriage. In the meantime, such marriages present us with a pressing pastoral need which can only be satisfied by reaching a common understanding.

Many people find it difficult to understand marriage as a sacrament and think of it as a mystification, a sacralization, a spiritualization or an idealization of marriage, of a kind that can hardly be expressed in the day-to-day experience of marriage. This giving of a higher, supernatural and even false value to marriage (which is often coupled with a shameful justification of the reality) is not without its dangers, because it can easily lead to giving a much lower value to the natural reality of marriage or even to isolating it altogether. It is really a question of including marriage as such, as a reality of creation, in the reality of Christ and regarding it as an effective sign of the salvation given by Christ.

2. THE ESSENCE OF THE SACRAMENTALITY OF MARRIAGE

(i) Marriage as the Sign of Christ

The bond or covenant of marriage has in itself an essential religious dimension. Even "natural" marriage is a religious symbol that points to God's faithfulness. This is why it was possible for the Old Testament authors to use marriage as the image and likeness of God's covenant with human beings. In Scripture, covenant is the reality of salvation as such. Salvation consists of God's definitive acceptance of man, his "yes" to humanity. It is God's communication of himself as love. God's "yes" really reaches people for the first time when they accept that "yes" in faith, hope and love and, in saying "yes" to God, respond to God in love. This unity in love existing between God and human beings is made present as a sign in marriage. It is realized in the highest and most unique way in Jesus Christ, in whom God said "yes" to human beings in a unique, definitive and unsurpassable way by communicating himself totally and making the humanity of Jesus the form of his existence in the world. On the other hand, Jesus opened himself completely to the reality of God even in his total obedience on the cross. In this way, he made himself, in his human self-surrender, the sign of the presence of God's love. [Jesus Christ is therefore in person God's covenant with people.] In him, God has once and for all time accepted everything human and has at the same time also affirmed it in its human dignity.

The marital love and faithfulness of those who are, through faith and baptism, "in Christ" are, in a very special way, included, borne up, purified and fulfilled by God's love and faithfulness in Jesus Christ. This situation is defined in the document on the Church of Vatican II in these words: "Authentic marital love is included in divine love and guided and enriched by the redeeming power of Christ and the Church's mediation of salvation."[46] [The love and faithfulness that Christian husbands and wives have for each other, then, are not simply the sign and symbol of the love of God—they are the effective sign, the fulfilled symbol and the real epiphany of the love of God that has appeared in Jesus Christ.]

If marriage represents a special form of being human in Christ that is based on baptism, it is also a special form of sharing in the death and resurrection of Christ. If marital love is seen as existing under the sign of Christ's cross, it must also be seen as being sustained by giving and being given, forgiving and being forgiven and a continuous process of new beginnings. Just as Christ loves the Church as a Church of sinners, purifies it and makes it holy, so too must married couples accept each other again and again with all their conflicts, in all their dissatisfactions and with all their guilt. This growth in love and this transformation are possible for married couples because they are able to have confidence that their human love and faithfulness are always surpassed and completed by the Easter victory of God over human lack of love and faithfulness.

It is possible to describe the participation of Christian marriage in the reality of Jesus Christ more precisely in both the negative and the positive sense.[47] The negative aspect was stressed above all by the theologians and canonists of the early Middle Ages, who defined marriage as a remedy against concupiscence. This definition strikes us as strange today, but it is possible to understand it when we remember the theological meaning of the term "concupiscence." It should not be thought of as synonymous with sensuality or sexual desire. It is, in the theological sense, the inner disintegration and fragmentation of human existence caused by sin—human sensuality insofar as it is opposed to the whole orientation of the person. It is as a remedy for this disintegration that the sacrament of marriage was defined by the early mediaeval theologians, who saw that marriage had a healing part to play in the integration of sex and eroticism into the whole human and religious structure of the individual and society. The beginning of a new creation is made by the sacrament of marriage.

This redemption from the "powers" of "flesh and blood" and their integration into the totality of human and Christian existence should make people free to serve God in his love (see 1 Cor. 6:20), that is, in their bodily and worldly relationships. This positive aspect can be described as the sanctification of those who are married. According to the New Testament, all those who are baptized are saints, that is, they have all been raised to the sphere of God's holiness (see 1 Cor. 1:2, 30; 6:11, etc.). The sacrament of marriage is in a special way a participation in the sanctifying service of Christ (see Eph. 5:26). This sanctification includes two elements: being taken into the service of God and his work in creation and redemption (*consecratio*) and being made inwardly capable of carrying out that service by sanctifying grace (*santificatio*).[48] Taken together, both of these aspects mean that married couples are, in their love for and faithfulness to each other, included in the love and faithfulness of God in Jesus Christ, with the result that their love for each other is an effective and fulfilled sign of the love of God. The life that man and wife share together in marriage therefore serves to glorify God. As M.J. Scheeben pointed out, sacramental marriage is not simply a symbol or an external example of the mystery of Christ and the Church, "but a copy of that mystery that has grown out of the union of Christ with the Church and is borne up by and penetrated with that union. Marriage does not merely symbolize that mystery. It really represents it in itself and represents it by showing itself to be active and effective in it."[49]

(ii) Marriage as the Sacrament of the Church

God's love and faithfulness in Jesus Christ applies to people in actuality. They are therefore present in human life in a visible and truly human way, that is, through the service of the Church as the community of believers. The love and faithfulness of God are made present by the love and faithfulness that Christians have for and towards each other. They are moreover, made present in this way in history. The

The Sacramental Dignity of Marriage · 37

Church is therefore the all-embracing sacrament of Christ, just as Christ himself is the sacrament of God.[50] What applies to the Church as a whole is concentrated in the sacraments and given its most complete form in them. What takes place in the sacraments, then, is not something that does not take place at all elsewhere in Christian life. The sacraments are, in other words, not an isolated and special sphere of activity. They are only capable of being fully understood and expressed as the supreme expression of what takes place in the rest of the life of the Church and its members.

Married and family life are in a very special sense the Church in miniature — Vatican II spoke of the family as the "domestic Church."[51] In this function, married and family life are not, however, simply a development of the essential being of the Church. They in fact make an active contribution to the building up of the Church. That is why married couples have a special charism, that is, a distinctive call, gift, and form of service, within the Church (see 1 Cor. 7:14). In a special way they contribute, by accepting and bringing up the children whom they are given, to both the internal and the external growth of the Church. They are also able to form living cells in the Church by the example of their life together as believers, and by the hospitality and openness of their "domestic Church."

The inner connection between marriage and the Church is most clearly expressed in the solemnization of marriage. It would be quite wrong to see this simply as an aspect of the Church's authority over marriage and as a formal duty that is justified by that authority. There has only been a formal duty of this kind in the Church since the appearance of the

Tridentine decree on marriage *Tametsi* in 1563.[52] What is more important in this context is that marriage is, because of its inner and essential being, not simply a private matter, but also a public and ecclesial matter. This public and ecclesial aspect of marriage means that it is most important for the couple to enter into marriage in the presence and with the active participation of the Christian community gathered together within the framework of the liturgy. According to the Catholic understanding of this matter, the active collaboration of the Church's office is required for the full and official constitution of a community of believers. This is the theological basis of the Church's ruling that marriage must be solemnized in the presence of a priest. The latter's task is, moreover, not purely formally legal. The questioning procedure and the acceptance of the consensus by the priest should be understood as a clarification of the ecclesial dimension of the marriage itself. The priest also makes that dimension clear by his function as the Church's official witness to the marriage, his proclamation of the word of God and his prayer over and blessing of the bride and bridegroom. In this way, the Church is as it were answerable to God in an official sense for the success of the marriage that has just been solemnized.

Even though the Church collaborates in the solemnization of marriage because this participation is in accordance with the essential being of marriage itself, Christian marriage nonetheless remains independent within the Church. According to the most widely accepted theological opinion, it is not the priest who bestows the sacrament of marriage, but rather the bride and bridegroom who give the sacrament to each other. Sacramental marriage, then, is founded on that personal act "whereby spouses mutually bestow and accept each other"[53] and their mutual consent constitutes the marriage. There is a difference between the Western Church and the Orthodox Church with regard to this aspect of Christian marriage that has persisted up to the present day. In the Orthodox Church, which has not experienced the separation between the Church and the world that has marked the theology of the Western Catholic Church since the twelfth century, the priest is regarded as the one who bestows the sacrament of marriage.[54] The Reformed Churches have a different view from both the Orthodox and the Western Catholic Churches. They were, because of their presuppositions regarding the reality of marriage, obliged to hand over the solemnization of marriage to the secular authorities.[55] This has led, in recent centuries, to a far-reaching process of secularization in the institution of marriage on the one hand and, at the same time, a privatization and spiritualization of the Christian life of married couples.

It is clear from the concepts used in connection with marriage that the difficult balance in the Catholic doctrine between the personal and the ecclesial elements has not yet been fully resolved. Traditionally, both aspects are expressed in the term "marriage contract."[56] It is, however, obvious that the legal term "contract" can only be applied to marriage in an analogous sense. It is especially since the rise of the individualistic and liberal theories of law in the eighteenth and nineteenth centuries that the term "marriage contract" has been open to misunderstanding. Several Christian authors have therefore argued that the term "institution" rather than "contract" should be applied to marriage.[57] There is no doubt that this term expresses more clearly than the word "contract" the fact that marriage is a reality that is previously given, that both embraces and transcends the partners and that is not simply placed arbitrarily at their disposal. The Second Vatican Council followed this linguistic usage and preferred to speak of the institution rather than the contract of marriage.[58] On the other hand, however, it cannot be denied that the word "institution" can be interpreted in various ways and can only be applied to marriage partially and analogously. The most suitable word, then, would seem to be the biblical term "covenant," which was also used in the documents of the Second Vatican Council. "Covenant" expresses the personal character of the consensus better than "contract" or "institution." It is also able to express the legitimate intention of marriage, its public character, which is contained in the term "contract." A covenant is both private and public. The covenant of marriage is not simply a personal bond or covenant of love—it is also a public and legal matter concerning the whole community of believers. This is, of course, why the covenant is normally concluded *in facie ecclesiae*.

This unity, dynamic tension and mutually complementary nature of the personal and the ecclesial aspects of marriage must go further than the simple act of solemnization and be worked out in the whole continued history of the marriage relationship.[59] This tension forms the basis both of the obligation that the married couple have to collaborate in the Church and the community and of the coresponsibility that the Church and the community of believers have with regard to the human and Christian success of the marriage in its early period and its later stages. In addition to its material and spiritual diaconate or ministry in the widest sense, one expression of which is marriage counselling, the Church also has a supportive function. In the present situation, pastoral work with families and the formation and strengthening of family groups are of fundamental importance in the task of revivifying the Church and its communities of believers and therefore in enabling it to carry out its mission in the world. It is also possible that attempts of this kind may form at least one step towards leading the Church and society as a whole out of the impasse into which they have in recent decades been drawn by an understanding of marriage and family life that has been one-sidedly based on the model of the individual partnership. Why should vital Christian communities consisting of family groups not take over at least some of the functions of the earlier extended family?

(iii) Marriage as an eschatological sign

This dynamic relationship that exists between the Church and marriage also has a further dimension. Neither the Church nor marriage exist in themselves. The Church always continues to be a sacramental sign and instrument and a symbolic anticipation of the gathering together and reconciliation of mankind at the end of time and the establishment of peace among the nations. Marriage too is a sign of eschatological hope. The festive mood at a wedding is a symbol of the joy and the fulfilment of human hopes that will be present at the end of time (see Mark 2:19ff; Matt. 22:1–14; 25:1–13 etc.). It is therefore not simply necessary from the human point of view alone to celebrate the wedding as festively as possible, it is also important to mark the occasion in this way as a hopeful anticipation and celebration in advance of the feast at the end of time.

Marriage, then, has the value of an eschatological sign, but there is also an eschatological reservation in the New Testament with regard to marriage (see Mark 12:25; 1 Cor. 7:25-38). Marriage belongs to the form of this world which is transient. According to Christian teaching, it is not an ultimate, but a penultimate and to that extent a temporary value. This eschatological relativization of marriage is not a fundamental devaluation—on the contrary, marriage is given a new content and meaning by being given a relative value in the eschatological sense. By being classified as a penultimate rather than as an ultimate value, marriage is demythologized, demystified and desacralized, and in this way its immanent beauty and inner wealth are more perfectly expressed. If, on the other hand, exaggerated expectations are projected onto marriage and the partners in marriage, the inevitable result is almost always disappointment. No partner can give the other heaven on earth. A person's urge to make such penultimate values absolute and his tendency to do violence to them in this way can only cease when he recognizes God as the ultimate reality. A person can only be fully human when he or she sees God fully as God. The eschatological glorification of God is the final humanization of humanity. The eschatological reservation regarding marriage is therefore the source of freedom in marriage. It binds both partners to God and prevents them from becoming enslaved to each other.

This eschatologically-based Christian freedom, however, presupposes that marriage is not the only possible call made by God to people or the only way in which people can be fulfilled.[60] The charism of the unmarried state is there precisely for the sake of this freedom in marriage (see 1 Cor. 7:7). A Christian who voluntarily remains unmarried for the sake of the kingdom of heaven (see Matt. 19:12) is not a better Christian than the one who marries. He or she does, however, express through the unmarried state an aspect that is essential for all Christians—he or she is there entirely for the Lord and his affairs (see 1 Cor. 7:32). He or she makes it clear, as a sign, through this eschatologically-based Christian freedom what the fundamental attitude of every Christian should be. According to the New Testament, then, this freely chosen unmarried state is an essential sign in the Church. The Church needs this sign at every period of its existence. It is also necessary for the success of Christian marriages.

Just as the Christian who remains unmarried for Christ's sake discloses the married Christian's freedom as a sign to the latter, so too does the eschatological character of marriage show the unmarried Christian that eschatological existence should not imply a flight from the world, but is in fact a special form of service in the world and for others. Both forms of Christian life have therefore to be understood in their mutual relationship. Each stands or falls with the other. A call to remain unmarried is a sign to the healthy Christian marriage, and a devaluation of the unmarried state is inevitably bound to lead to a distortion of Christian values in marriage. Both aspects of Christian life must therefore be borne in mind in any responsible pastoral policy for marriage.

Chapter III

The Unity and Indissolubility
of Marriage

1. JESUS' WORDS ABOUT UNCONDITIONAL
FAITHFULNESS

The unity and indissolubility of marriage cannot be
justified on the basis of the sacramental nature of the reality; they are in the first place founded on the anthropological
character of marriage as such. The act in which the bride
and bridegroom give and receive each other has in itself an
inner tendency towards definitiveness and exclusiveness (we
dealt with this aspect in the first chapter). The person who
gives himself or herself to another no longer belongs to
himself or herself but to the other. The marital bond of
faithfulness is therefore, on the basis of its inner being,
disposed to be definitive and exclusive. This is why the Old
Testament authors regarded the unity and indissolubility of
marriage as being based in the order of creation itself (see,

for example, Gen. 2:24). This unity and this indissolubility, already an essential part of marriage as a reality of creation, are given an ultimate and unambiguous meaning in the Old Testament by the insertion of the order of creation into God's plan of salvation. God's faithfulness to his people is a constant theme throughout the Old Testament (see, for example, Exod. 34:6; Ps. 99:5, etc.). Faithfulness in marriage is therefore an image of God's faithfulness in the covenant. (This was discussed in the second chapter.) Adultery, on the other hand, was regarded by the Old Testament authors as a symbol and an effect of unfaithfulness to God (see, for example, Hos. 4:2; Jer. 3:6ff, 7:9; Ezek.23).

It is against the background of the Old Testament theology of the covenant that the statement in Deuteronomy 24:1-4 about the drawing up of a bill of divorce should be understood.[61] What is involved in this text is not permission for divorce — this is simply assumed — but a prohibition of the remarriage of the divorced wife, since this is an "abomination before the Lord." What is at stake, then, is the holiness of the people of the covenant. It was not until the later period of Judaism that the idea of permission for divorce was derived from this passage in cases where the husband found some "scandal" in his wife. This regulation provided the wife with a certain amount of legal protection, since her husband could not send her away for any arbitrary reason or in a sudden upsurge of passion. He could only dismiss her in accordance with a certain legal formality. All that was open to dispute was whether the rather vague criterion of what was "scandalous" in the wife's behaviour should be interpreted more severely or more leniently. It would seem, however, that even within the Old Testament itself there was criticism of the practice of divorce (see, for example, Mal. 2:14-16; Ecclus. 7:26).

It was Jesus who first replied unambiguously to the question of the indissolubility of marriage.[62] According to Mark 10:2-12, Jesus was asked the controversial question by the Jews: "Is it lawful for a man to divorce his wife?" Jesus' reply was very typical of the nature of his proclamation. He did not reply directly to the question; in other words, he did not say what was or what was not permitted. As long as such questions were asked, attempts were made to limit God's will and to obtain as much as possible for oneself as a result. What Jesus wanted above all to do, however, was to express God's will, which had already been made manifest in creation, in all its radical and unconditional nature. It was therefore not enough for a marriage or a divorce to be legally valid in the presence of a lawyer. What was at stake for Jesus was the very heart of humanity. Hence, "Every one who looks at a woman lustfully has already committed adultery with her in his heart" (Matt. 5:28).

This was such an astonishingly radical point of view that it is not difficult to understand the disciples' statement: "If such is the case of a man with his wife, it is expedient not to marry" (Matt. 19:10). Indeed, such a bond between man and wife for better or for worse could well become an unbearable burden and an excessive demand. Jesus' words can therefore only be understood if they are viewed within the context of his whole proclamation. He did not want to impose intolerable burdens on his fellows or make demands on them that they could not fulfil. His message of the coming of the kingdom of God was concerned above all with what God does with people and for them. What a person does is simply his or her response to God's action. This, then, is not an abstract law, but God's will to save people. It was, according to Jesus, God who joined man and wife together, thereby creating a bond that was not available to humanity. This bond was not a burden, but a grace embedding the human bond of faithfulness in God's faithfulness.

Jesus' words clearly do not form an article of Christian law or a kind of excessive moral demand. It would therefore be wrong to speak in this context of an ideal commandment. No, his words here are a prophetic, messianic and effective affirmation of God's saving activity and an invitation to make use of the possibility offered by God. This offer of grace can be rejected, but God's grace continues to exist and becomes a judgment, accusing humanity of hardness of heart. If, however, the offer is accepted in faith, God's covenant becomes a way of salvation and it is possible for the human covenant of marriage to continue in strength on the basis of the covenant between God and humanity, which the partners can bear constantly in mind and use as a landmark by which to take their bearings again and again throughout their married life and as a point of departure from which to make new beginnings. God's covenant is also a protection for a wife. By it, she is no longer — as the Pharisees' question presupposed — at the mercy of a man's decision. She has security in the decision of God and in his covenant. Jesus' words about the indissolubility of marriage therefore form the basis of a new understanding of marriage as a partnership, in which neither partner is at the mercy of the other, but both are at God's mercy in faith.

A straight line can be traced from these words of Jesus in the synoptic gospels to the statement in the letter to the

Ephesians (Eph. 5:31ff), in which the bond of faithfulness between man and wife in marriage is justified on the basis of the unconditional faithfulness of the covenant between Christ and the Church. The indissolubility of marriage is therefore not based exclusively on a law of the Church, nor is it simply a moral norm or a metaphysical principle. It is rooted in the sacramentality of marriage itself. Since the covenant of marriage makes God's covenant in Jesus Christ sacramentally present, adultery is not primarily a sexual failing for the Christian, but an offence against the person's being in Christ.

Augustine's doctrine of the bond of marriage, which he developed and which determined the whole tradition of the Church with regard to marriage, can be reinterpreted against this background.[63] This doctrine has often been presented in objective ontological categories, with the result that the impression has sometimes been given that the bond of marriage is a kind of metaphysical hypostasis that is placed above marriage in the concrete. One constantly valid "matter" is expressed in this presentation, which is otherwise insufficient and open to serious criticism, since the personal covenant between the married couple creates a constant ontological reality of an intersubjective kind that transcends the personal level. The covenant therefore creates a "bond" that has to be understood not as an objective reality, but rather as in accordance with the personal sphere of marriage (we said something about this question in Chapter I). God's covenant receives this human reality, confirms it and deepens it. God's covenant, which is not available to mankind, makes the covenant of marriage similarly not available. Adultery therefore means that a Christian, in

The Unity and Indissolubility of Marriage · 49

committing it, is arrogating to himself or herself a power that he or she does not possess and is at the same time deceiving the new partner by giving something that does not belong to him or her and cannot therefore be given.

It should be clear from what we have said so far that the doctrine of the sacramental bond of marriage does not in any sense give a totally legal structure to marriage. On the contrary, the doctrine is an ontological expression of the lasting aspect of promise and grace contained in sacramental marriage. It points to the constant claim that the partners can make on each other and their openness to each other. It follows therefore that a husband and wife who are separated have a constant duty to forgive each other and an unquenchable hope of reconciliation. This duty and this hope may perhaps go contrary to human experience. In faith, however, we may accept that God's love and faithfulness in Jesus Christ never cease, even if human love and faithfulness are broken.

2. THE PRACTICE OF THE CHURCH IN SCRIPTURE AND TRADITION

(i) The biblical tradition

Jesus' words about unconditional faithfulness in marriage were spoken, like the whole of his message, within the context of the expectation of the imminent coming of the new era. This expectation was fulfilled in an unexpected way by the cross and resurrection of Jesus and the outpouring of the Holy Spirit. The kingdom of God, proclaimed by Jesus Christ, became a reality in the paradoxical form of the cross. Although the new creation became a reality in the baptized through the Holy Spirit, the earlier era continued in a certain way, and the hardness of heart, for which Jesus criticized the Jews, was found among his own disciples. Marriage, which belonged both to the earlier order of creation and to the new order of salvation, was the place where the two overlapping eras came into contact with each other and where there were inevitably repeated tragic conflicts. The post-paschal Church had to look, in the Spirit of Jesus Christ that had been given to it, again and again for new orders in which, on the one hand, the eschatological demand made by Jesus would be fully preserved and, on the other, the concrete situation would also be fully taken into account. This task was clearly recognized from the very beginning. Hardly any other statement has been handed down to us in the New Testament in so many different ways as Jesus' statement about the impossibility of divorce. This shows that the Church from the very beginning understood Jesus' words not as a kind of article of the law, but as prophetic and messianic words.

The evangelist Mark added an instruction to the disciples (10:10-12) to Jesus' dispute with the pharisees about divorce (10:1-9). Most exegetes regard this additional passage as a community tradition, in which the originally prophetic words of Jesus were transmitted in the form of a communal institution. This is expressed in its oldest form in Luke 16:18: "Everyone who divorces his wife and marries another commits adultery and he who marries a woman divorced from her husband commits adultery." This logion presupposes that only the husband can dissolve the marriage and clearly points to Judaeo-Christian communities. The situation is different in Mark. He presupposes the Roman law, according to which the wife also had a right to divorce. He therefore added: "If she divorces her husband and marries another, she commits adultery" (10:12). We find in the New Testament, then, a dynamic adaptation of the Church's law to changed circumstances in society.

The Matthaean clauses referring to unchastity or adultery were clearly attempts to overcome another transitional situation.[64] The prohibition of divorce is provided with an appendix: "except for unchastity" (Matt. 5:32, 19:9). The interpretation of this appendix is disputed and it is therefore not possible to come to any far-reaching or fundamental conclusions. The interpretation that is most probably correct is the one that views these clauses against the background of the Judaeo-Christian communities as presented in such texts as Acts 15:20, 28. These communities tried to express the Old Testament ideal of holiness in a very radical way. They recognized the will of God in separation from a partner who was living in "qualified" unchastity, that is, incest, prostitution, sexual perversity, lasting adultery, and so on. (See, for example, Lev. 18:19–22; Deut. 24:1–4.) The clauses therefore are not concerned with an exceptional law giving the right to remarry. They are, on the contrary, concerned with the right and even the duty to separate "for the sake of God." This is not a concession, but an accentuation of the Torah that is fully in accordance with the whole tendency of Matthaean teaching. Even if it were a question of a concession, however, we would be bound to ask how this could claim to be valid in the later Church and this problem could not be solved by exegetical methods alone. The later Church has to express the words of Jesus in a way that is in accordance with the situation in which it finds itself, just as Matthew had to for his communities.

Whereas Matthew had to deal with a Judaeo-Christian situation, Paul was concerned with relationships between Christians and pagans. In 1 Corinthians 7:10-15, he attempts to deal with the problem of marriages between them when the unbelieving partner is not prepared to live in peace with the Christian. What is interesting and of fundamental importance is that Paul was aware of the authority of the word of the Lord excluding divorce and that he nonetheless, on his own authority, introduced a certain praxis of divorce in the situation in which the Corinthian community found itself. This shows that Paul, in common with all the New Testament authors, regarded the word of the Lord not as a rigid and isolated law, but as the expression of God's saving will in Jesus Christ addressed to people in whatever situation they found themselves.

A Christian is therefore not necessarily restricted in such cases. Permission to remarry in accordance with the later Pauline privilege is admittedly not given unhesitatingly. In the background there is the fact that a Christian should not even eat at table with a partner who gives scandal because of (qualified) unchastity (see 1 Cor. 5:1f, 9-13), but that there should be no definitive rejection (see 1 Cor. 5:5; 2 Cor. 2:5-11). What is normative in every such case is God's will to save. God makes it possible for husband and wife to separate for the sake of peace, but he makes reconciliation the supreme norm (see 1 Cor. 7:11-15).

The whole of the New Testament bears witness to the unconditional nature of Jesus' words. At the same time, however, all the evidence in the New Testament points to the fact that the Church has to understand and realize those words not legally, but spiritually. The Spirit of Jesus Christ is the Spirit of Christian freedom, which is manifested not in

The Unity and Indissolubility of Marriage · 53

self-seeking arbitrary decisions, but in selfless love, peace and reconciliation. It is therefore the Church's constant task to understand and realize the Word of Jesus Christ in the Spirit of Jesus Christ.

(ii) The Tradition of the Church

Paul had to deal with the problem of mixed marriages between Christians and pagans, and later on similar problems arose within the Christian communities themselves.[65] In faithfulness to Jesus' teachings, new solutions had to be found. From the very beginning, then, the binding force of Jesus' words was constantly in the minds of the Fathers of the Church. Since even remarriage after the death of the first partner was forbidden, a second marriage while the first partner was still alive was clearly excluded.

Although this was fundamentally the attitude of most of the Church Fathers, a relatively flexible practice in the Church is evident from the statements made by some of the Fathers, at least with regard to those who had married again after a divorce in which they were the innocent party. All that we can do here is to point to a few aspects of this situation. The first writer of importance to deal with this question was Origen (d. 253/254), who reported that certain leaders of the Christian community had permitted women whose husbands had committed adultery and who were therefore divorced from them in some cases to remarry during the lifetime of their first husbands.[66] Origen was aware that this praxis was contrary to the teaching of Scripture, but regarded it as quite reasonable, because it helped to prevent a worse situation from arising. A hundred years later, Basil (d. 379), who was also conscious that the practice went against Scripture, appealed to the Church's common law whenever he readmitted a man who had been divorced because of his wife's adultery and had remarried after a long period of penance to the community of the Church and let him once again participate in the eucharist.[67] He believed that it was not possible to say with certainty whether a woman who was cohabiting with a man who had been deserted by his first wife was an adulteress. She should, he believed, be treated leniently and not condemned, as should a man in the same position.[68]

There was no such common law in the Western Church, but there are a number of indications in the writings of the Western Fathers of a more flexible praxis. In the fourth century, Ambrosiaster[69] and later Augustine (d. 430) made reference to this. The latter spoke in one place, which he later corrected, of a "pardonable error."[70] During the turbulent period at the end of the ancient world and the beginning of the Middle Ages, attempts were made by several of the Church's synods[71] and in the Irish and Anglo-Saxon and Frankish penitential books[72] to do justice in certain cases to the reality of the situation in marriage by tolerating or even permitting a second marriage while the first partner was still alive, but was, for example, lost, missing or in prison. To maintain the ideal of Christian marriage, the practice of penance was used as a means.

The situation, then, was tense, but unambiguous.[73] The most fundamental aspect of the Church's tradition is unconditional faithfulness to Jesus' teaching. The Church did not recognize any other tradition or any exceptional law or casuistry. Two possibilities were not open to the Church's law. Because of its very being, the Church could only express

The Unity and Indissolubility of Marriage • 55

the will of God as revealed in Jesus Christ. Nonetheless, the difficult human situations in which the reality of marriage was involved in the world with its "hardness of heart" and from which individual Christians could hardly escape presented the Church with problems with no easy solutions. The validity of Jesus' words could not be restricted, but Christians placed in such situations could not be condemned. There was, according to the Fathers, only one possiblity and that was to exercise tolerance and leniency and not to condemn, so that a worse situation did not arise. What they expressed, in other words, was that it was a question of something that was in itself impossible. On the other hand, however, according to the Fathers, God always made it possible for a person who was prepared to be converted and did what was possible for people to lead not only a human existence, but also a Christian existence within the Church. This was not contrary to the will of God to which the Church bore witness, since, according to the gospel, God's will was not an abstract factor, but his unconditional intention to save every person in whatever situation he or she found themselves, a will that was revealed in Jesus Christ. It was the Church's task to be in accordance with this actual will of God made manifest in Christ.

The practice of the Church and the difference between that practice in the East and the West developed on the basis of this understanding of tradition. In the Eastern Church,[74] for certain objective reasons which were based on a loose analogy between adultery and death, it became normal practice to permit remarriage, in accordance with the principle of economy, although the second marriage was not placed on the same level as the first. This practice does not violate the principle of indissolubility as such. What it does in fact is to provide the Christian who is ready to do penance, on the basis of God's mercy, with a new possiblity of a human and Christian life within the Church in certain difficult situations. This is why the liturgy in the Eastern Church for a second marriage is dominated by the theme of penance.[75]

In the Western Church, on the other hand, partly as a consequence of the Decree of Gratian (d. 1279), a much stricter praxis became established in the second millennium.[76] In the second century, however, even the Catholic Church did not take over Jesus' universal prohibition of divorce without making some attempt to differentiate and to find compromises for human hardness of heart and weakness. The decision to terminate the community of married life—separation from bed and board—marks a certain compromise with regard to Jesus' demand.[77] In the early Middle Ages, the so-called Pauline privilege was inferred from 1 Corinthians 7:12ff, permitting the partner who had become a Christian to put an end to a marriage contracted before his baptism and to remarry if the partner who remained a pagan refused to live in peace with the Christian partner.[78] (This interpretation went far beyond the original meaning of the Pauline text.) At the beginning of the modern era, when the Church was confronted in the mission field with completely new polygamous situations, the so-called Petrine privilege was similarly used. According to this privilege, the pope was able, under certain circumstances, to separate the bond of nonsacramental marriages *in favorem fidei*.[79] This practice has been extensively applied throughout the present century, although it has scarcely been possible to justify it theologically. [What it means in fact is that the absolute indissolubility of marriage in the Catholic Church only applies to sacramentally concluded marriages and even in such marriages only to those that have been validly solemnized and physically consummated.[80]]

It should therefore be clear that the Catholic tradition in marriage in the second millennium — even since the Council of Trent — has not been so uniform as it has often been presented. The only marriage that the Church recognizes as absolutely indissoluble is a sacramental marriage that has been validly concluded and physically consummated.[81] What is more, even such respected sixteenth century theologians as Cajetan and Ambrosius Catharinus interpreted the Matthaean clauses on unchastity as exceptions to Jesus' universal prohibition of divorce.[82]

This historical evidence has led many authors today to ask whether the Church cannot do more than it is at present doing and indeed whether it cannot separate even sacramentally concluded marriages.[83] This modern conclusion, however, places an excessive demand on the historical argument, which can, by its very nature, never be regarded as absolutely certain and will always be disputed in the questions that we are considering here. This demand is being made by those who are confusing individual pieces of traditional evidence with tradition in the dogmatic sense. The latter, however, is the result not only of individual fragments of evidence, but also, and above all, of agreement over a long period about this and other evidence. This agreement is to be found in the case that we are considering here, most importantly in the Church's need to express the unconditional will of God as revealed in Jesus Christ not as a rigid law, but as God's promise of salvation. The conclusion drawn by those who are today asking the Church to separate sacramentally valid marriages is based on a reversal of the order of priority in the Church's role. These theologians are attributing to the Church, in other words, a power that is fundamentally opposed to its real power to serve the Gospel. In its attempt to do justice to the evidence of tradition, the Council of Trent followed a very different course.

(iii) The teaching of the Council of Trent

[The obligatory teaching of the Church about the indissolubility of marriage was defined by the Council of Trent (1545-1563).[84] This definition was preceded by the decision of the "Union" Council of Florence (1439-1445).[85] The immediate reason for returning to this question at Trent was Martin Luther's criticism of the teaching and practice of the Catholic Church.[86]

Luther criticized the Roman Church above all for what he believed was its presumption in ascribing to itself a competence of this kind in matrimonial matters. In his opinion, the Church had no power either to permit or to prohibit divorce. In this, however, he continued to insist on the indissolubility of marriage. In the case of adultery and in the analogous case of 1 Corinthians 7:15, where one partner behaves in such a pagan fashion that he or she deserts the other forever, Luther exhorted the innocent party to accept the freedom of a new marriage. The contrasting practice of the Catholic Church was, in his opinion, tyrannical and opposed to the freedom of the Gospel. Luther's criticism, then, was clearly concerned not only with the isolated question of the indissolubility of marriage, but also with the fundamental relationship between the Gospel and the Church, the right interpretation of Christian freedom and the question of the sacramental nature of Christian marriage that was related to this.

The Tridentine answer to these questions was not simple. On the one hand, the Council had to reject Luther's fundamental attack on the Catholic understanding of the Church. On the other hand, however, the Fathers of the Council were familiar with the clauses on adultery in the Gospel of Matthew and with the leniency expressed in many of the patristic texts. It was therefore out of the question that patristic teaching should be condemned by the Council. What is more, highly respected conciliar theologians such as Cajetan and Ambrosius Catharinus put forward another interpretation of the Matthaean clauses. There was also the practical problem that there was a kind of church union between the Latin hierarchy and the Orthodox population and their priests on the Mediterranean islands ruled by Venice, and divorce and remarriage were practised on those islands in accordance with Orthodox custom. For political reasons, the Venetians did not want this custom to change. As in many other cases, the Council had therefore to make sure that the false teaching in question was unambiguously condemned, while at the same time not restricting freedom within the Church and in theology.

Long discussions preceded the decree that was finally promulgated on 11 November 1563 during the twenty-fourth session. In the proem of the definitive text, reference is made to the Old and New Testaments and the indissolubility of marriage is at once discussed. In the various canons that follow, what is stressed is the competence of the Church to lay down a legal order. Canon 7 is particularly important in this context: "Who says that the Church errs when it taught and teaches that, according to the evangelical and apostolic doctrine, because of the adultery of one spouse, the bond of marriage cannot be dissolved and that both, also the innocent party, who has not given cause for adultery, cannot contract another marriage while the other spouse is still alive and that he commits adultery who, after dismissing the adulterous wife, marries another and she who, after dismissing the adulterous husband, weds another: may he be excluded."[87]

This is a complicated statement, but the following data emerge if it is interpreted in the light of what has been said above. [Firstly, the indissolubility of marriage forms part of the obligatory testimony of the New Testament. Secondly, marriage is not simply a matter which only concerns the private and individual sphere of Christian freedom. As a sacrament it is also a matter of the Church. The Church therefore has the right to lay down a legal order with regard to marriage that is in accordance with the Gospel. Thirdly, the traditional and existing teaching and practice, according to which divorce and remarriage are not possible in the case of adultery, is not erroneous, but is, on the contrary, in accordance with the teaching of the New Testament.] What is meant by "in accordance with" here is that this is not simply a question of church discipline, but also, and above all, a question of an obligatory teaching and practice inspired by the Gospel, even though, according to the linguistic usage of the period during which the council took place, this was not an ultimately obligatory dogma in the modern sense of the word, but an obligatory teaching and practice in the wider sense of the word, a teaching and practice that was justified by and based on the revelation of Christ. On the other hand, however, it is also relevant that the conciliar text speaks not of an identity between the evangelical doctrine and the teaching and practice of the Church, but only of an "accordance." This more open form was clearly intended to avoid a condemnation of the teaching of many of the church Fathers and the practice of the Eastern Church.

It is clear, then, that the Council of Trent taught unambiguously the indissolubility of marriage, but that it did not intend to summarize or systematize the whole of the Church's tradition or to provide an all-embracing doctrine of the indissolubility of marriage. The only intention was to come to a decision in the controversy that had been raging at the time between the Catholic Church and the Lutherans. Controversies within the Catholic Church itself were, however, left open. No previous decision of any kind was therefore made by the Council of Trent with regard to the pastoral problems of the twentieth century. All that the council has done to further the solution of these problems in an obligatory way is to provide us with a number of essential points of view. The Tridentine decision does not, however, release the Church from its obligation to look again and again, within the constantly changing historical situation, for a legal order in marriage that is in accordance with the Gospel.

3. CONTEMPORARY PASTORAL PROBLEMS

It is noticeable that, in the past, the problem of divorce has always arisen when the Church is at a transitional stage in a new period of history or a new form of society. The problem arose, for example, in the case of Matthew and Paul at the transitional phase between the Judaeo-Christian and pagan Christian communities. In the case of Origen and Basil, it arose when the Church was becoming a greater Church of the people. Divorce also became a problem in the early Middle Ages, a period of transition from the later ancient world to the Germanic form of society and again in the sixteenth century, when Western missionaries encountered the cultures of Asia and South America.

Once again, the Church finds itself in a similar transitional situation. It was pointed out at the Second Vatican Council that mankind is now on the threshold of a new dynamic and historically orientated epoch,[88] which has, because of its greater degree of mobility, already led to greater instability in marriage. Marriage has, in fact, lost almost all its social supports. Civil law, which has an influence on human moral consciousness that should not be underestimated, recognizes a relatively wide spectrum of reasons for divorce and the attitude in society as a whole towards the phenomenon of divorce and consequent civil remarriage is characterized not simply by tolerance, but rather by indifference and even approval. It is therefore easy to understand in this current situation that divorced persons who have contracted a new civil marriage have come to regard this as more or less accepted behaviour and to believe that they have a right to marry again. Many of those who have divorced and married again have experienced human suffering in their first marriage, but happiness in the second. Others, however, have found that divorce and remarriage have led to suffering, because they are contrary to God's order, but, especially when new moral obligations have resulted from the civilly contracted second marriage (children, for example), have not been able to change the new situation. It is these who are in need of pastoral help because their situation is most difficult. As yet, no solution that is in every way satisfactory has been found for this urgent pastoral problem.[89] What is more, no solution is suggested in this chapter. All that I can do here is to discuss fundamental points of view that must be borne in mind in any consideration of the problem.

The first point of view is based on the fact of unconditional faithfulness to Jesus' words, which apply not only to the partners in marriage, but to the Church's law and pastoral practice in the Church. The Church is not able to formulate its own casuistic law that is different from the law of Christ. It can only be faithful to the words of Jesus. It cannot simply pay lip-service to its confession of the indissolubility of marriage and undermine it in practice. It therefore cannot recognize a second marriage that has been contracted civilly during the life of the first partner as having either equal value as the first marriage or as being a sacrament. If it were to do so, it would diminish its own value as a sign and would not be giving man the service that it owed to him in the present situation. The Church is, after all, almost the only relevant reality in society today that has the moral authority to represent this fundamentally Christian faithfulness in marriage and to stand up for any children of a marriage, the existence of which may be endangered. The law by which the Church protects the indissolubility of marriage is as such a "law of mercy" and Christians ought therefore to cease to play justice and mercy off against each other in this matter.

The second of these three fundamental points of view does not contradict the first theologically. It is, on the contrary, closely linked to it. Jesus proclaimed the God of human beings; his proclamation of the indissolubility of marriage was not a killing law, but a word of life and salvation. His message is therefore an obligation to the Church to care for existing marriages, both those that are safe and those that are threatened. This also includes legal protection. If the Church's law in the Spirit of Christ is a law of mercy, then it is also essential for the Church to question itself again and again to make sure if it is doing justice to people in all the difficult and complex situations in which they find themselves in the modern world or whether it is not helping them in those situations. It may, for example, be an obstacle to their conversion and reconciliation, rejecting them hurtfully instead of giving them human and Christian support. A revision of canon law might well help, for instance, in the many cases in which there was, according to our interpretation of the relationship based on contemporary psychological insights, no full act of personal consent to the marriage contract because the partners were lacking in maturity, to open the way to an annulment of such marriages. We are also bound to ask how a second marriage following a validly solemnized and sacramental first marriage should be judged from the human and Christian point of view. In this case too, it is important to do justice to the actual human situation. According to the rules of traditional moral theology, the actual situation or *circumstantiae* must be taken into consideration in judging the moral quality of an action. In the case of marriage breakdown today, in which divorce and remarriage may be involved, these cir-

The Unity and Indissolubility of Marriage · 65

cumstances include the attitude prevailing in contemporary society. Taking these into account does not mean, of course, that the contemporary attitude should be unquestioningly justified. It does mean, however, that we have to be very careful when we judge the objective guilt of a person who acts on the basis of this late twentieth-century attitude. In pastoral care, we have not only to encounter a person in this difficulty on the basis of a fundamental standpoint — we have also to see the whole person in his or her actual situation as a whole. The dynamic tension between these two standpoints should be retained very carefully.

The third and most energetically disputed point of view is concerned with our theological evaluation of a civilly contracted second marriage which takes place while the first partner is still alive. In considering this difficult question, we must begin by stating what is certain in the light of Scripture and the Church's tradition. It is this. Whatever may be the case with regard to the subjective guilt of the parties or party concerned, objectively a second such marriage represents a contradiction to the order established by God. The first marriage has become a permanent part of the history of the person or persons in question. It can be humanly broken by adultery when this takes place, but it cannot simply be cancelled out. A second marriage during the lifetime of the first partner cannot therefore be regarded as equal in status to the first marriage, nor can it be seen as a sacramental representation of the new covenant.

We are, however, bound to ask whether a second marriage is therefore simply valueless both anthropologically and theologically. To find an answer to this question, it is helpful to remember that a certain hierarchy of forms of marriage is recognized in present canon law. If this were not so, it would not be possible for an invalid Christian marriage to be subsequently made valid by withdrawing the legal effects (*sanatio in radice*)[90] or for a marriage that has been validly contracted but not physically consummated (*matrimonium ratum non consummatum*)[91] to be dissolved. Finally, it can be pointed out that a civilly contracted second marriage is not regarded in canon law as concubinage or as a similar relationship.[92] What is given greater recognition is the presence of a genuine desire to marry. A civil marriage of this kind may include essential human values such as friendship, love, faithfulness and the duty to care for each other,[93] and these values are often inspired by a genuinely Christian attitude to faith. Whenever faith is present in the second, civilly contracted marriage, and is expressed in love and is made effective in penance for the guilt incurred by the breaking of the first marriage, then the second marriage also participates in the spiritual life of the Church. As the one and universal sacrament of salvation, the Church is also at the same time the Church of sinners. The Church is realized in different grades and the seven sacraments represent the supreme form of this realization (see, for example, below, Chapter IV).

The answer to this very controversial question can perhaps be expressed most clearly by means of a comparison. A broken marriage is not simply cancelled out. It continues to exist, even though it can be compared with a ruin. It is therefore not possible to replace it with a second marriage equal to the first. What is possible, however, and in many cases necessary for survival, is some kind of emergency accommodation. This image would seem to be in

The Unity and Indissolubility of Marriage · 67

accordance with the way in which God acts in the history of human salvation. He often writes straight on crooked lines. It is on the basis of this point of view that the Church constructed its order of penance in the past—God does not let us perish after the shipwreck of sin, but he also does not simply allow us to board a comfortable new ship. What he does is to offer us the plank of penance so that we can save our lives.[94] A third comparison may also help us to understand this problem. Guilt wounds us and the wound does not simply disappear. It forms a scar[95] and such scars are lasting signs that can hurt again, but they allow us to go on living a humanly fulfilled life that may be all the more mature because of suffering.

These images, then, point to possible ways of preserving the lasting reality of the first marriage and therefore the continued existence of the Christian bond of marriage on the one hand and of recognizing, on the other, the human and Christian values of a second civilly contracted marriage in cases where people are prepared for conversion and reconciliation and do what is humanly possible in their situation.

We cannot go into the pastoral consequences of these three points of view in detail here, but must turn to the pressing theological question of whether divorced persons who have remarried should be admitted to the sacraments of the Church.[96] This is not a question that can be answered by one individual theologian or pastor, since participation in the sacrament of penance and the eucharist is the sign *par excellence* of full membership of the visible community of the Church. It is a question of fundamental importance that has to be decided ultimately by the pastoral office of the

Church. It cannot, moreover, be left to the personal decision of the married persons themselves. Legal and pastoral rules or guidelines are required and these must be clear, unambiguous and possible for everyone to understand.

According to the present structure officially approved in the Church, it is not permissible for remarried divorced couples to receive the sacraments unless they are in danger of death or are living together as "brother and sister." This ruling is justified by the claim that a second marriage of this kind contracted while the first partner is still living is objectively in contradiction to Jesus' teaching and is also a cause of public scandal; sacramental marriage is moreover regarded by the Church as the only legitimate framework for a sexual relationship. If the Church, then, does not want to lose its credibility, it cannot give its official approval to such marriages by admitting the partners to the sacraments. Such an action would obscure their value as signs and this would in turn weaken the support that the Church has to give both to healthy and to endangered marriages. This does not mean, of course, that Christians living together as man and wife in a second, civilly contracted marriage are written off, as it were, by the Church or in the religious sense. Even if they are prevented from belonging to the full eucharistic community, they can take part in many different ways in the religious life of the Church. They have, in practice, the status of penitents, in the sense in which the word was used in the early Church, and are able to take part in the service of the word in the Church, and the rest of the church community has the special task of interceding and caring for them.

Many Christian theologians and pastors—including

myself—believe that the facilities for pastoral help are insufficient in the present situation and that not enough provision is made for them in canon law as it stands now.[97] Generally speaking, they do not advocate, of course, that a second marriage should receive a liturgical blessing or be solemnized sacramentally, thus putting it on the same level as the first marriage. Such an action could not be reconciled with the whole tradition of the Church. The more moderate authors who have written about this question therefore believe in a policy similar to the practice of "tolerance" and "leniency" that emerges from many documents of the early Church and similar to (though not identical with) the practice of the Eastern Church, which was not formally excluded by the Council of Trent and which also amounts to an order of penance. The God proclaimed by Jesus Christ reveals to all men, including sinners, when they turn back to him, a possibility of salvation.

The Church should act in accordance with God's way of acting and for this reason, it should be possible to admit divorced people who have remarried to the sacraments on three conditions: 1) when they are sorry for their guilt and have made amends for it as well as they can; 2) when everything humanly possible has been done to achieve reconciliation with the first partner; and 3) when the second marriage has become a morally binding union that cannot be dissolved without causing fresh injustice.

A solution of this kind would seem at least to do justice to the teaching of Jesus, the complexity and difficulty of the situation in which such people often find themselves today and the human and Christian values that may well be present in a civilly contracted second marriage. It ought to be possible to avoid both giving scandal to others and causing indifference in those concerned by following a sensible and responsible pastoral policy which makes it clear that all men are in need of conversion and reconciliation and that no one has reason to point critically at others. Such a programme ought also to lead to a deepening of the spiritual life of the community as a whole, especially with regard to the need for conversion and reconciliation.

These theological considerations cannot, of course, establish norms for pastoral activity. They are, however, necessary in view of the complex pastoral situation today, in which theological understanding is of great importance. This is, after all, from the point of view of theology at least a question that is not simply already resolved. It is rather subject to the ultimate decision of the Church's pastoral office. This final decision can only be made in accordance with the whole Church. In this decision making, two points of view must have the highest priority: a renewal and a deepening of our understanding of the human and Christian value of faithfulness in marriage and a renewal and deepening of our need for penance and of the Church's order and practice of penance. Both of these viewpoints are concerned ultimately with God's faithfulness, by which human faithfulness is sustained and made holy and which also remains faithful to people when they become unfaithful and, by means of conversion, offers them a possibility of salvation. Avoiding rigidity on the one hand and laxity on the other, the Church has the task of bearing witness to this divine faithfulness as God's way of saving all people. It is only in this way that it can act in accordance with Jesus' words and practice.

Chapter IV

Christian Marriage in Contemporary Society

1. THE RELATIONSHIP BETWEEN CHURCH AND CIVIL MARRIAGE

In the history of mankind, marriage has always existed in many forms and at many levels and its dynamic reality has included divine and human laws, personal and objective relationships, and private and public aspects.[98] These different elements remained more or less closely fused together for as long as society as a whole was marked by religious values. The modern process of secularization and civil marriage (made possible by secularization) have, however, created an entirely new situation here. The consequences of this new situation for our understanding of the sacramental character of marriage are only now becoming really clear to us.[99]

This situation can only be understood if it is recognized

Christian Marriage in Contemporary Society • 73

that one of its roots is to be found in the mediaeval doctrine and, in particular, in the canonistic theory of the sacramentality of marriage, according to which a marriage is constituted exclusively by the consensus or mutual consent of the bride and bridegroom. These two teachings set marriage free from its close links with the sacral clan framework. Marriage was personalized by this theory of mutual consent and this led to the abuse of clandestine marriages, that is, marriages based exclusively on the mutual promise made by the bride and bridegroom and without any public form. The aim of the Tridentine decree *Tametsi* (1563) was to remove this abuse by introducing an obligatory church form. This attempt on the part of the Church, however, to correct the abuse led in turn to the solemnization of marriage being dominated by the Church, a practice which was quite contrary to the early and the mediaeval tradition of the Church. It was not until the civil form of marriage was introduced as an obligatory legal condition by modern secularized states that an alternative was provided. The introduction of the civil ceremony, however, meant that Catholics, who were still obliged to marry according to the church form of marriage, had in fact to submit to a double solemnization of marriage. The relationship between the civil and the church marriage therefore became a problem.

A solution to this problem that proved unacceptable to the Catholic Church was provided by the theory of the absolute authority of the State, as manifested in France by Gallicanism and in Austria by Josephinism.[100] The marriage contract, as a matter of civil law, was made subject to the exclusive competence of the State, while the sacrament, which was seen fundamentally as a blessing, was placed within the authority of the Church. Certain court theologians regarded the contract of marriage merely as a prior condition for the sacrament and the sacramental sign as contained in the priest's blessing. According to this understanding of marriage, the sacrament was added to the marriage contract proper. The unity existing between the order of creation and that of redemption, which is fundamental to the sacramentality of marriage, was in this way cancelled out. These ideas were rejected by various popes[101] and, according to canon law, there could be no valid contract of marriage among baptized persons that was not *eo ipso* a sacrament.[102] This meant that the Church refused to allow baptized Catholics to take part in the civil marriage ceremony, both in its optional and in its obligatory form.[103] It is a naive assumption that this refusal was based on fear of losing influence in society. On the contrary, it was based on a genuine pastoral intention, since the obligatory civil marriage could easily lead to the belief that the marriage contract was a purely secular matter and the church marriage was no more than an additional blessing that could easily be allowed to lapse. The so-called thesis of identity protected the sacramentality of marriage from becoming a kind of pious superstructure on marriage. The civil form of marriage that evolved from the secularization of society, on the other hand, could and did lead to a secularized understanding of marriage.

Although there were many fully justified and indispensable concerns that were at the root of the Church's critical attitude towards the obligatory form of civil marriage, we are bound to ask today whether many of the arguments used by the Church have not become anachronistic. This is particularly so in view of the fact that the relationship between the Church and the State is nowadays especially not marked by hostile opposition or indifferent coexistence, but by amicable partnership. This modern relationship is to a great extent the consequence of the stress placed by the Second Vatican Council on the autonomy of the secular sphere.[104] The council clearly emphasized, moreover, that this understanding was not simply the result of contemporary thinking—it arose from the very nature of creation itself. In fact, the breakdown of unitarian order that prevailed in the Middle Ages led to a clearer understanding of this truth.

What, then, are the practical consequences of this truth for our evaluation of civil marriage? Thomas Aquinas stressed the dignity (*honestas*) of marriage, which was based, not only on the sacramental nature of the relationship, but also on the human values contained in it (friendship, faithfulness, love, mutual care, and so on).[105] The identity of the contract and the sacrament of marriage has therefore to be understood as a dynamic unity that is in itself differentiated. From the purely philosophical point of view, this identity, which in its definition is more than a mere tautology, presupposes a certain differentiation. This becomes apparent in the unity that exists between the order of creation and that of redemption. It would obviously be heretical to insist on an identity without differentiation here. That is why the relationship between the reality of creation and that of salvation must be seen in marriage as unadulterated and undivided.

If what I have said so far is taken seriously, the relationship between civil and church marriage no longer has to be regarded as one of hostile oppposition or indifferent coexistence. They are different but related realities and together they are able to express the many different aspects of the one marriage contract.[106] Present canon law recognizes that the state has the task of dealing with the civil consequences of marriage, such as entitlement to name, property, and inheritance.[107] It is certainly not in the Church's interest to concern itself even indirectly with questions of this type by accepting responsibility for some form of optional civil marriage. On the other hand, the modern and ideologically neutral State (even if it represents certain fundamental Christian values) cannot give sufficient material content to marriage. It can only protect it and lay down the legal forms that will act as norms for its civil and legal validity.

It is at this point that the Church has a social service to perform. Understood in the correct sense, this is not an additional service. On the contrary, it expresses a dimension that is essential to Christian marriage, so essential indeed that without it a marriage between Christians cannot be fully valid. Church marriage and civil marriage, seen in this light, form a single whole which can achieve inner completion for Christians only with the form prescribed by the Church and which can therefore only be recognized as canonically valid and as sacramental with that form.

In theory, the Church ought to be able to return today to a situation similar to that before the promulgation of the Tridentine decree *Tametsi* and make it possible for its members to choose either a civil marriage, which was at that time recognized as valid and sacramental, or a church marriage. Although this solution has been suggested by many specialists in the field, however, there are good pastoral reasons for rejecting it. One of the most important is that a civil marriage in modern secularized society is not the same as a marriage contracted in an earlier society existing before the Enlightenment and thinking of itself in principle as religious. In this instance, Luther presupposed an understanding of the State that was not that of the modern world. The philosophically neutral State cannot, however, give an inner meaning to marriage. The civil marriage ceremony was therefore bound to lead to a secularization of marriage and consequently to marriage's becoming gradually emptied of meaning or else to its becoming an exclusively private affair of the partners. This, however, is in contradiction to the Christian understanding of marriage both as a public affair and as a service that the Church owes to married couples. For this reason, we ought now to have a very open attitude towards civil marriage and its human values, while at the same time regarding church marriage as an important public sign of faith in the readiness of married couples to be united in the Lord.

2. MARRIAGE AS A SACRAMENT OF FAITH

Many problems, some of them new, have arisen as a result of the secularization of society and human attitudes. Only a few of these problems can be discussed in this final section and then only in the light of their effect on the pastoral care of marriages. What is fundamentally at stake is this: how can the Christian view of marriage in the secularized situation be made intelligible, and how can that view be translated in the concrete into practice in the Church? Like all the other sacraments, marriage is also a sacrament of faith. It can therefore only be entered into in faith as a sacrament and it can only be lived in the Christian sense from the experience of faith. This living faith cannot, however, in the contemporary situation, be presupposed or taken for granted.

The many baptized but nonpractising Catholics who do not value the religious content of a church marriage and are therefore satisfied with a civil ceremony present the Church with a problem. How should such marriages be assessed? Certainly they cannot be regarded as canonically valid, but this does not mean that they are valueless from the human and Christian point of view. In any attempt to solve this problem, it is important to remember that, according to canon law, a purely civil marriage can be recognized as canonically valid if it is cured at its root (*sanatio in radice*) on the basis of the present will to marriage.[108] What is recognized, in other words, is the existence of a human will to marriage, a phenomenon that distinguishes a civilly contracted marriage from simple concubinage. It is, however, difficult to reconcile this with another ruling, according to which each of the two partners of such a civil marriage are able, after divorce, to enter into another marriage, contracted in Church. This is a serious cause of scandal for both Christians and non-Christians because of the gulf it reveals between the Church's law and its moral teaching. Most people rightly believe that the Church should, in its law, protect the human values of civilly contracted marriages. Even if the Church is unable to recognize such marriages as canonically valid, it ought to take care that no one should come, by means of an injustice (the guilty dissolution of a civilly contracted union), to a sacramental marriage in the Church. It is, in this context, worth considering whether, in this case,

Christian Marriage in Contemporary Society · 79

there should not be a "contemporary" impediment to marriage, similar to the impediment of "crime," according to which no one should be able to come to a new marriage by murdering the first partner.[109] The Church ought, in cases such as this, to be able to stand up for people and their rights.[110]

Let us continue a little further in this direction. Since all reality exists in Jesus Christ, and God wants all men and women to be saved in him, he is the head of all people, and God's grace is offered to everyone in him and in every human situation. In the Church as the universal sacrament of salvation, then, there are many stages and degrees of realization, from that of those who do not believe but are in good faith to that of Catholic Christians in a state of sanctifying grace.[111] All human will to marriage is therefore an imperfect realization of the mystery of Christ and his Church, which strives to realize itself more and more perfectly. This may therefore be particularly important if, for one reason or another, a sacramental church marriage is not possible, but a will to marriage, which is both human and Christian, is really present, as is frequently the case with those who have divorced and are remarried. Such partners should trust in God to give them the grace to fulfil their duties as a married couple, since their union is a participation in the mystery of Christ and the Church because of their faith, which is expressed as penance for their guilt incurred in the breaking of their first marriage.

We must now briefly consider another pastoral problem: What happens when a baptized, but nonpractising Christian enters into a church marriage, perhaps, for example, for human or social reasons or because it is a more festive form of ceremony, but who does not give his consent to its inner meaning? Would it be advisable in such a case to recommend that marriage should be delayed (a parallel situation to delayed baptism)? In other words, should the church marriage be deferred and a purely civil ceremony be advised? Is it possible for a priest in an extreme case even to refuse to solemnize a church marriage? This problem is particularly pressing in our modern secularized society and it points to a need to define the relationship between faith and sacramentality.

The point of departure that is traditionally taken by Catholic theologians in this case is the identity of the canonically valid and the sacramental marriage. According to this theory of identity, every canonically valid marriage is *eo ipso* also a sacramental marriage. An objection that has often been raised against this theory, however, is that the sacrament is, according to this identity, interpreted automatically and even magically. This objection is, however, based on a misunderstanding of the Catholic doctrine of the sacraments. There can be no automatic sacrament and there can be no sacrament without faith. A distinction is made in Catholic sacramental theology between the objective validity of the sacrament in question that is based on its "objective" expression (*ex opere operato*) and the person's fruitfulness in grace which presupposes a certain subjective disposition (*opus operantis*). An integral aspect of the "objective" fulfilment of the sacrament is the presence of at least a minimal intention in the giver and in the receiver of the sacrament.[112] Since the bride and bridegroom give each other in marriage and are therefore each at the same time givers and receivers, they must both have the intention, as an integral element of their consensus or mutual consent, of entering into their marriage in the Lord. If not, neither a canonically valid nor a sacramental marriage takes place.

What does this intention consist of? According to the traditional teaching of the Church,[113] it does not need to be consciously present at the moment; all that is required is that it should be virtually present. It must, however, not be purely externally orientated towards the performance of external actions under the customary circumstances (the place, time, dress, and so on). Nor does it need to be a special or deeply reflected intention; in other words, it does not have to be explicitly directed towards the administration of the sacrament and towards the aim and effect of that sacrament. It is sufficient to have a general and direct intention to do what Christians are in the habit of doing in the rite in question. If this understanding of the intention is applied to the sacrament of marriage, it amounts to this: the bride and bridegroom do not need to have the intention of giving and receiving a sacrament of the Church by means of the marriage contract. It is enough for them to have the intention of marrying in the way in which Christians marry. This will to marriage includes the intention to receive the sacrament of marriage as long as it is not explicitly denied.[114]

Obviously, this is a minimal definition and in no sense an expression of an ideal of faith and intention in marriage. Even according to this minimal definition, however, there can be no valid and sacramental marriage without at least a minimum of faith. Two conclusions can be drawn from this. In the first place, the Church has to do everything possible, by its proclamation of faith in the context of preparation for marriage and at the marriage ceremony itself, to arouse an understanding in faith of the fulness of the sacrament of marriage. It is not enough, if the sacrament is to be fully effective, for the partners to be given a minimal instruction about what constitutes a valid marriage. The aim must be a real deepening of the Christian meaning of marriage. In the second place, it seems important that the church marriage should be delayed in the case of couples who, despite all attempts based on pastoral concern, do not give their consent explicitly to the minimal conditions outlined above. This can, of course, only happen in marginal cases. Normally it must, in the absence of evidence to the contrary, be assumed that couples who want to be married in church will have the right intention. A deferment of the church marriage can, after all, only be considered after an intensive application of pastoral care. If the church marriage has, however, eventually to be deferred and the bride and bridegroom have a marriage which is not valid in the eyes of the Church, but which is honourable because of its human values, no injustice is done to them, at least in a highly secularized and therefore increasingly tolerant society. Above all, honesty is satisfied.

In conclusion, I should like to point briefly to the pastoral consequences of these dogmatic considerations. Because the situation in which marriage and the other Christian sacraments have been placed has changed radically in recent years, we have tended to speak more explicitly than in the past of a sacrament of faith and to recognize that a considerable pastoral task is involved in the administration of the sacraments generally and the sacrament of marriage in particular. This pastoral work includes preparation for marriage (for engaged couples and others), marriage counselling, the formation of marriage and family groups, and education in the Christian view of marriage by preaching, catechesis, work among young people and adults, and in publications. It is also of pastoral importance to find the best possible form for the liturgical celebration of the wedding itself. If some measure of success is achieved in this pastoral work, it is likely that the present crisis may become an opportunity to reach a fuller and deeper human and Christian understanding of marriage. This must be the aim of all attempts to reform our pastoral practice.

This pastoral policy in marriage cannot be treated in isolation. It is really an emergency case in which the foundations of Christian faith as a whole have to be considered (see above, Chapters I and II). In Christian faith, human beings make a total decision in favour of God, who, in Jesus Christ, made a total decision in favour of human beings. God's unconditional love and faithfulness makes our unconditional love and faithfulness possible. Christian marriage is an actualization of Christian life lived in "faith working through love" (Gal. 5: 6). An intensification of faith is therefore the most important service that can be performed; it is the real content and aim of this and every other form of pastoral work.

Notes

1. See G. Schmidtchen, *Zwischen Kirche und Gesellschaft. Forschungsbericht über die Umfragen zur Gemeinsamen Synode der Bistümer in der Bundesrepublik Deutschland* (Freiburg, Basle & Vienna, 1972) pp. 12-19; J. Gründel, "Kirche und moderne Wertsysteme," *Befragte Katholiken—Zur Zukunft von Glaube und Kirche. Auswertungen und Kommentare zu den Umfragen für die Gemeinsame Synode der Bistümer in der Bundesrepublik Deutschland*, ed. K. Forster (Freiburg, Basle & Vienna, 1973) pp. 67-70.

2. See Vatican I, *DS* 3016 (39); Vatican II, Pastoral Constitution *Gaudium et Spes*, 3ff, 10ff, 22, 40, 42ff, 62, etc.

3. See the survey in H. Schelsky, *Soziologie der Sexualität. Über die Beziehungen zwischen Geschlecht, Moral und Gesellschaft* (Hamburg, 1955); F.X. Kaufmann, "Die Ehe in sozialanthropologischer Sicht,"*Das Naturrecht im Disput,* ed. F. Böckle (Düsseldorf, 1966) pp. 15-60; J. F. Thiel, "The Institution of Marriage: An Anthropological Perspective," *Concilium* 5 (1970), pp. 13-24; D. Claessens, "Institution Ehe in einer sich wandelnden Gesellschaft. Soziologische und anthropologische Aspekte," *Ehe und Ehescheidung,* (Munich, 1972) pp. 75-83.

4. See *Das Naturrecht im Disput*, op. cit.; J. David, *Das Natur-recht in Krise und Läuterung* (Cologne, ²1969); *Naturrecht in der Kritik,* ed. F. Böckle & E.W. Böckenförde (Mainz, 1973).

5. See *Summa Theologiae*, Suppl. 41, 1.

6. Ibid., ad 3.

7. Ibid., 42, 2; 65, 2.

8. Ibid., 91, 4.

9. J. Freisen, *Geschichte des kanonischen Eherechts bis zum Verfall der Glossenliteratur* (Paderborn, ²1893; reprinted Aalen, 1963); R. Sohm, *Das Recht der Eheschließung. Aus dem deutschen und kanonischen Recht geschichtlich entwickelt* (Weimar, 1875; reprinted Aalen, 1966); a summary of this book appeared in H. Dombois, *Kirche und Eherecht. Studien und Abhandlungen 1953-1972* (Stuttgart, 1974), pp. 19-71; G.H. Joyce, *Die christliche Ehe. Eine geschichtliche und dogmatische Studie* (Leipzig, 1934); P. Adnès, *Le Mariage* (Tournai, 1961); E. Schillebeeckx, *Marriage: Secular Reality and Saving Mystery* (London & Melbourne, 1965); the articles by E. Hillman, K. Ritzer, N. van der Wal and P. Delhaye in *Concilium* 5 (1970), pp. 25-38, 67-75, 76-82, 83-88.

10. H. Schelsky, *Soziologie der Sexualität,* op. cit., p. 34.

11. See Augustine, *De bono coniugali* XXIV, 32: *PL* 40, 394; *De genesi ad litteram,* IX, 7, 12: *PL* 34, 397; Thomas Aquinas, *Summa Theologiae*, Suppl. 49, 1ff. The doctrine of the three goods of marriage was taken up officially by the Council of Florence (*DS* 1327), Pius XI, in his Encyclical *Casti Conubii* (*DS* 3703ff), Vatican II, Pastoral Constitution *Gaudium et Spes*, 48.

12. See J. Höffner, *Ehe und Familie. Wesen und Wandel in der industriellen Gesellschaft* (Münster, 1959); H. Begemann, *Strukturwandel der Familie. Eine sozialtheologische Unter-suchung über die Wandlung von der patriarchalischen zur part-nerschaftlichen Familie* (Hamburg, 1960); "The Humanization of Sexuality," *Concilium* 5 (1970), pp. 155-71; W. Dreier, "Zur Situation von Ehe und Familie in unserer Gesellschaft — sozialwis-senschaftliche Analysen und Perspektiven," *Berichte und Dokumente. Zentalkomitee der deutschen Katholiken*, 22,

pp. 20-63; F. Böckle, "Das Unwandelbare im Wandel — theologisch-sozialethische Thesen zu Ehe und Familie in unserer Gesellschaft," *Berichte und Dokumente*, 22, pp. 64-76. Hegel pointed to the dialectical tension between marriage and modern middle-class society (discussed in Section I 2) and described it, with reference to Sophocles' Antigone, as tragic. See Hegel, *Grundlinien der Philosophie des Rechts*, § 154ff; *Phänomenologie des Geistes*, ed. Hoffmeister, p. 318ff, 339ff.

13. M. Horkheimer, "Autorität und Familie," *Kritische Theorie*, 1 (Frankfurt, 1968), p. 350. J. Habermas has also recently thrown light, from the standpoint of neo-Marxism, on the importance of the family for hominization. See his *Zur Rekonstruktion des Historischen Materialismus* (Frankfurt, 1976), p. 148ff.

14. See the *Codex Iuris Canonici*, canon 1081 § 2.

15. *Catechismus ex decreto Concilii Tridentini* II, 8, 13: *Prima igitur est haec ipsa diversi sexus naturae instinctu expetita societas, mutui auxilii spe conciliata, ut alter alterius ope adiutus vitae incommoda facilius ferre, et senectutis imbecillitatem sustentare queat.*

16. See *DS* 3707.

17. Pastoral Constitution *Gaudium et Spes*, 48ff. H. Doms made a valuable contribution to the renewal of our understanding of marriage, at least in the German-speaking countries, even before the Second World War; see his *Vom Sinn und Zweck der Ehe* (Breslau, 1935), and *Gatteneinheit und Nachkommenschaft* (Mainz, 1965). For the debate on the subject, see J. Leclercq & J. David, *Die Familie. Ein Handbuch* (Freiburg, 1955), p. 18ff; A. Auer, *Weltoffener Christ. Grundsätzliches und Geschichtliches zur Laien-frömmigkeit* (Düsseldorf, 1960), p. 213ff.

18. See the Encyclical *Humanae Vitae*; see also *Enzyklika "Humanae Vitae" über die rechte Ordnung der Weitergabe menschlichen Lebens* (Nachkonziliare Dokumentation 14) (Trier, 1968); see also the pronouncement made by the German bishops with regard to pastoral care after the publication of *Humanae Vitae* in 1968.

19. This direction is clearly indicated in the German bishops' pastoral letter on human sexuality (*Hirtenbrief der Deutschen Bischöfe zur Frage der menschlichen Geschlechtlichkeit*, 30 April 1973) and the declaration made by the Synod of German bishops on Christian marriage and family life ("Christlich gelebte Ehe und Familie," *Gemeinsame Synode der Bistümer in der Bundesrepublik Deutschland. Offizielle Gesamtausgabe* 1 (Freiburg, Basle & Vienna, 1976), pp. 423–57; see also the working paper on the form and meaning of human sexuality ("Sinn und Gestaltung menschlicher Sexualität," ibid., Freiburg, Basle & Vienna, 1977).

20. Pastoral Constitution *Gaudium et Spes*, 25.

21. See J. Pieper, *Über die Liebe* (Munich, 1972); B. Welte, *Dialektik der Liebe. Gedanken zur Phänomenlogie der Liebe und zur christlichen Nächstenliebe im technologischen Zeitalter* (Frankfurt, 1973); E. Biser e.a., *Prinzip Liebe. Perspektiven der Theologie* (Freiburg, Basle & Vienna, 1975).

22. This total view of human sexuality means that the Augustinian tradition will inevitably have to be corrected. In this tradition, sexuality has been excluded from the sphere of human spirituality and from the understanding of man as made in the image of God. See Augustine, *De Trinitate* XII, 7, 12: *PL* 42, 1005. For the totally personal aspect of human sexuality, see U. Ranke-Heinemann, "Die geschlechtliche Grundbefindlichkeit des Menschen," *Handbuch der Pastoraltheologie* II/1 (Freiburg, Basle & Vienna, 1966), pp. 38–54). See also E. Michel, *Ehe. Eine Anthropologie der Geschlechtsgemeinschaft* (Stuttgart, 1948); G. Scherer, *Ehe im Horizont des Seins* (Essen, [2]1967); J. and I. Splett, *Meditation der Gemeinsamkeit. Aspekte einer ehelichen Anthropologie* (Freiburg, 1970).

23. Thomas Aquinas was therefore able to call the *bonum fidei* a *pars iustitiae* (Suppl. 49, 2 ad 3, 5, 7). It was above all Hegel who emphasized the fact that love and justice belonged closely together; see his *Grundlinien der Philosophie des Rechts*, § 30, 36, 48, 57. See also W. Pannenberg, *Was ist der Mensch? Die Anthropologie der Gegenwart im Lichte der Theologie* (Göttingen, [2]1964), p. 67ff.

24. See especially H. Schelsky, *Soziologie der Sexualität*, op. cit., pp. 11-15, who followed A. Gehlen & H. Plessner here; see also F.X. Kaufmann, in *Das Naturrecht im Disput*, op. cit., pp. 20-26.

25. See S. Freud, *Das Unbehagen in der Kultur* (*Discontent in Civilization*) (Frankfurt & Hamburg, 1971), pp. 85ff, 92ff.

26. See especially Hegel, *Grundlinien der Philosophie des Rechts* (*Philosophy of Right*), § 173; see also J. Leclercq and J. David, *Die Familie*, op. cit., pp. 16-24; A. Auer, *Weltoffener Christ*, op. cit., p. 213ff. For a (one-sided) criticism of the traditional Church position, see F.W. Menne, *Kirchliche Sexualethik gegen gesellschaftliche Realität* (Munich & Mainz, 1971).

27. Thomas Aquinas, *Summa contra gentes* IV, 78.

28. See especially M. Scheler, A. Portmann, A. Gehlen and H. Plessner; see also the summary in W. Pannenberg, *Was ist der Mensch?*, op. cit., pp. 5-13.

29. See J.B. Metz, "Freiheit," *Handbuch Theologischer Grundbegriffe* I (1962), p. 411ff. See also W. Kasper, "Die Verwirklichung der Kirche in Ehe und Familie," *Glaube und Geschichte* (Mainz, 1970), p. 336ff.

30. See F. Nietzsche, "Genealogie der Moral" (*Genealogy of Morals*), *Werke* 2, ed. S. Schlechta, (Munich, 1955), p. 799.

31. See G. Marcel, *Geheimnis des Seins* (*Mystère de l'Etre*) (Vienna, 1952), p. 472.

32. See G. Marcel, *Sein und Haben* (*Etre et Avoir*) (Paderborn, 1954), pp. 15, 19, 43ff, 102ff, 129, and *Homo Viator. Philosophie der Hoffnung* (Düsseldorf, 1949), pp. 132-72, 173-86. See also B. Welte, "Miteinandersein und Transzendenz," *Auf der Spur des Ewigen* (Freiburg, Basle & Vienna, 1965), pp. 74-82.

33. For the relationship between the fundamental human situation and the sacrament, see W. Kasper, "Wort und Symbol im sakramentalen Leben. Eine anthropologische Begründung," *Bild-Wort-Symbol in der Theologie*, ed. W. Heinen (Würzburg, 1968), pp. 157-75; Kasper, "Wort und Sakrament," *Glaube und Geschichte*, op. cit., pp. 285-310.

34. Karl Barth elaborated—rather one-sidedly—the connection

between man's having been created in the image of God and creation as man and woman; see his *Kirchliche Dogmatik* (*Church Dogmatics*), III/1, pp. 204-33; III/2, pp. 344-91. See also C. Westermann, *Genesis* (*Bibl. Kommentar AT*, I/1), (Neukirchen and Vluyn, 1974), pp. 208ff, 220ff, 306-22.

35. For the sacramentality of marriage, see H. Volk, *Das Sakrament der Ehe*, (Münster, ²1956); K. Rahner, "Die Ehe als Sakrament," *Schriften zur Theologie* VIII, (Einsiedeln, Zürich & Cologne, 1967), pp. 519-40; J. Ratzinger, "Zur Theologie der Ehe," *Theologische Quartalschrift* (1969), pp. 53-74 (*Theologie der Ehe*, (Regensburg and Göttingen, 1969), pp. 81-115); W. Kasper, "Die Verwirklichung der Kirche in Ehe und Familie," *Glaube und Geschichte* (Mainz, 1970) pp. 330-54; M. Schmaus, *Der Glaube der Kirche* II (Munich, 1970) pp. 491-531; D. O'Callaghan, "Marriage as Sacrament," *Concilium* 5 (1970), pp. 101-10; W. Beinert, "Die Ehe als Sakrament der Kirche," *Beiträge zur Theologie der Ehe*, (Kevelaer, 1971), pp. 11-36; K. Reinhardt, "Sakramentalität und Unauflöslichkeit der Ehe in dogmatischer Sicht," K. Reinhardt and H. Jedin, *Ehe—Sakrament in der Kirche des Herrn* (*Ehe in Geschichte und Gegenwart* 2) (Berlin, 1971), pp. 7-59; K. Lehmann, "Zur Sakramentalität der Ehe," *Ehe und Ehescheidung*, (Munich, 1972) pp. 57-72; E. Christen, *Ehe als Sakrament—neue Gesichtspunkte aus Exegese und Dogmatik* (*Theologische Berichte* 1) (Einsiedeln, 1972) pp. 11-68; L. Boff, "The Sacrament of Marriage," *Concilium* 7 (1973), pp. 22-33; L. Duss-von Werdt, "Theologie der Ehe. Das sakramentale Charakter der Ehe," *Mysterium Salutis* IV/2, pp. 422-49; H. Volk, "Von der sakramentalen Gnade der Ehe," *Christus alles in allen* (Mainz, 1975) pp. 70-95. See also the works by P. Adnès and E. Schillebeeckx, op. cit., in note 9.

36. See H. Baltensweiler, *Die Ehe im Neuen Testament. Exegetische Untersuchungen über Ehe, Ehelosigkeit und Ehescheidung* (*Abhandlungen Theol. AT. und NT.* 52) (Zürich & Stuttgart, 1967) pp. 43-81; R. Schnackenburg, "Die Ehe nach dem Neuen Testament," *Theologie der Ehe*, ed. G. Krems and

R. Mumm (Regensburn & Göttingen, 1969), pp. 40-55; H. Greven, "Ehe nach dem Neuen Testament," *Theologie der Ehe.* op. cit., pp. 40-56; P. Hoffmann, "Jesus' Saying about Divorce and its Interpretation in the New Testament Tradition," *Concilium* 5 (1970), pp. 51-66; R. Pesch, *Freie Treue. Die Christen und die Ehescheidung* (Freiburg, Basle & Vienna, 1971) pp. 22-32. See also J. Ratzinger, "Zur Theologie der Ehe," op. cit., p. 54ff.

37. See H. Baltensweiler, *Die Ehe im Neuen Testament*, op. cit., pp. 218-35; R. Schnackenburg, *Die Ehe nach dem Neuen Testament*, op. cit., p. 25ff; H. Schlier, *Der Brief an die Epheser* (Düsseldorf, 1957) p. 262ff; J. Gnilka, *Der Epheserbrief (Herders Theologischer Kommentar zum Neuen Testament* X, 2) (Freiburg, Basle & Vienna, 1971) p. 274ff; G. Bornkamm, "*Mysterion*," *ThWNT* IV, p. 829ff.

38. See *DS* 1799; the Council of Trent does not argue on the basis of Scripture so much as on a suggestion (*innuit*) of Scripture.

39. H. Volk, "Ehe," *LThK* III (^{2}1959), p. 681.

40. Second Lateran Council (1139): *DS* 718; Council of Verona (1184): *DS* 761; Innocent III (1198-1216): *DS* 769, 793; Second Council of Lyons (1274): *DS* 860; John XXII (1318): *DS* 916; Council of Florence (1439-1345): *DS* 1327; Council of Trent (1545-1563): *DS* 1801; Pius IX, *Syllabus* (1864): *DS* 2965-2974; Leo XIII, Encyclical *Arcanum divinae* (1880): *DS* 3142 f; Pius X, Decree *Lamentabili* (1907): *DS* 3451; Pius XI, Encyclical *Casti Connubii* (1930): *DS* 3700, 3710ff; Second Vatican Council, Pastoral Constitution *Gaudium et Spes*, 48

41. See Martin Luther, "De captivitate Babylonica ecclesiae" (1520): *WA* 6, p. 550ff; summarizing p. 553: *Sit ergo Matrimonium figura Christi et Ecclesiae, sacramentum autem non divinitus institutum, sed ab hominibus in Ecclesia inventum.* For the contemporary Protestant attitude towards marriage, see W. Lohff, "Die Ehe nach evangelischer Auffassung," *Ehe und Ehescheidung. Ein Symposium* (Stundenbücher, 30), (Hamburg, 1963), p. 53. It is not without significance that most Protestant theologians deal with the subject of marriage not within the

framework of dogmatic theology, but as an ethical question. (See, for example, the writings of W. Elert, K. Barth, E. Brunner, H. Thielecke, P. Althaus, W. Trillhaas and others.) M. Thurian, in *Mariage et célibat* (*Foi vivante*, 135) (Neuchâtel, 1964), is exceptional among Protestants in his attitude towards marriage. See also "Ehe," *Religion in Geschichte und Gegenwart* II (^{3}1958), p. 322ff; *EKL* I (1956), pp. 1001–1003; *Lexikon für Theologie und Kirche* III (^{2}1959), p. 698ff (bibliography). It is not possible for me to go into the many problems of mixed marriages in this context; the reader should consult R. Beaupère and others, *Die Mischehe in ökumenischer Sicht* (Freiburg, 1968); P. Lengsfeld, *Das Problem der Mischehe. Einer Lösung entgegen* (Freiburg, Basle & Vienna, 1970).

42. Martin Luther, "Ein Traubüchlein für die einfältigen Pfarrherrn" (1529): *WA* 30, III, 74.

43. Martin Luther, "Von Ehesachen" (1530): *WA* 30, III, p. 205.

44. Martin Luther, "Ein Traubüchlein" (1529): *WA* 30, III, p. 75ff.

45. Martin Luther, *Tischreden*, No. 233.

46. Dogmatic Constitution on the Church, *Lumen Gentium*, 11; see also *DS* 1799.

47. See the synthesis in Thomas Aquinas, Suppl. 42, 3.

48. For this distinction, see H. Volk, "Das Wirken des Heiligen Geistes in den Gläubigen," *Gott alles in allem. Gesammelte Aufsätze* I (Mainz, 1961), p. 90ff.

49. M.J. Scheeben, *Die Mysterien des Christentums*, ed. J. Höfer (*Gesammelte Schriften* II) (Freiburg, 1951), p. 496.

50. Vatican II defined the Church as a "sacrament of intimate union with God and of the unity of all mankind, a sign and an instrument of that union and unity" (Dogmatic Constitution on the Church, *Lumen Gentium*, 1). See also the works of O. Semmelroth, K. Rahner, and E. Schillebeeckx. A good summary will be found in L. Boff, *Die Kirche als Sakrament im Horizont der Welterfahrung. Versuch einer Legitimation und einer strukturfunktionalistischen Grundlegung der Kirche im Anschluß an das II. Vatikanische Konzil* (Paderborn, 1972).

51. Dogmatic Constitution on the Church, *Lumen Gentium*, 11.

52. See *DS* 1813-16. See also K. Mörsdorf, "Die Eheschließung nach dem Selbstverständnis der christlichen Bekenntnisse," *Münchener Theologische Zeitschrift* 9 (1958), pp. 241-56; R. Lettmann, *Die Diskussion über die klandestinen Ehen und die Einführung einer zur Gültigkeit verpflichtenden Eheschließungsform auf dem Konzil von Trient* (Münster, 1967); H. Dombois, *Kirche und Eherecht. Studien und Abhandlungen 1953-72* (Stuttgart, 1974), pp. 117-34.

53. Pastoral Constitution, *Gaudium et Spes*, 48.

54. See H. Dombois, *Kirche und Eherecht*, op. cit., pp. 197-213.

55. See Martin Luther, "Von Ehesachen" (1530): *WA* 30, III, p. 207.

56. See the *Codex Iuris Canonici*, canon 1012 § 2. See also U. Mosiek, *Kirchliches Eherecht unter Berücksichtigung der nachkonziliaren Rechtslage* (Freiburg, ^{2}1972), pp. 35, 42.

57. J. Leclercq and J. David, *Die Familie*, op. cit., pp. 32-37; H. Dombois, *Kirche und Eherecht*, op. cit., pp. 84-95.

58. Pastoral Constitution, *Gaudium et Spes*, 47ff.

59. See F. Böckle, F. Betz and N. Greinacher, "Die Ehe als Vollzug der Kirche," *Handbuch der Pastoraltheologie* 4 (Freiburg, Basle & Vienna, 1969), pp. 17-94; *Ehe und Familie (Pastorale* 2), (Mainz, 1973).

60. See M. Thurian, *Mariage et célibat* (Neuchâtel, 1964); E. Gössmann, "Ehe und Ehelosigkeit. Eine Literaturübersicht," *Bibel und Leben* 9 (1968), pp. 230-36.

61. See G. von Rad, *Das fünfte Buch Mose* (*Alt Testament Deutsch* 8), (Göttingen, 1964), p. 107ff. For the Jewish praxis of divorce, see Strack and Billerbeck, *Kommentar zum Neuen Testament aus Talmud und Midrasch*, I (Munich, ^{3}1961), p. 312ff; H. Baltensweiler, *Die Ehe im Neuen Testament*, op. cit., p. 37ff; K. Schubert, "Ehescheidung im Judentum zur Zeit Jesu," *Theologische Quartalschrift* 151 (1971), pp. 23-27.

62. See, in addition to the book and articles listed in note 36,

F. Hauck and S. Schulz, *"Porne,"* *Theologisches Wörterbuch zum Neuen Testament* VI (1959), p. 590ff; J. Dupont, *Mariage et divorce dans l'Evangile,* (Bruges, 1959); E. Schweizer, *Das Evangelium nach Markus* (*Neues Testament Deutsch* 1) (Göttingen, 1967), p. 114ff; G. Bornkamm, "Ehescheidung und Wiederverheiratung im Neuen Testament," *Geschichte und Glaube* 3/1 (Munich, 1968), pp. 56-59; K.-H. Schelkle, *Theologie des Neuen Testaments* 3 (Düsseldorf, 1970), p. 241ff; K. Haacker, "Ehescheidung und Wiederverheiratung im Neuen Testament," *Theologische Quartalschrift* 151 (1971), pp. 28-38; R. Schnackenburg, "Die Ehe nach der Weisung Jesu und nach dem Verständnis der Urkirche. Geschichtlich Bedingtes und bleibend Gültiges," *Ehe und Ehescheidung,* ed. F. Henrich and V. Eid (Munich, 1972), pp. 11-34; G. Lohfink, "Jesus und die Ehescheidung," *Biblische Randbemerkungen,* ed. H. Merklein and J. Lange (Würzburg, 1974), pp. 207-17; A. Kretzer, "Die Frage: Ehe auf Dauer und ihre mögliche Trennung nach Matt. 19: 3-7," ibid., pp. 218-30.

63. See Augustine, *De nuptiis et concupiscentia* I, 10, 11; 17, 19; 21, 23: *PL* 44, 419ff, 424ff, 427; *De bono coniugali* III, 3; VII, 6-7: *PL* 40, 375, 378.

64. In addition to the earlier Catholic books and articles mentioned in note 62 and the article by F. Hauck and S. Schulz in *Theologisches Wörterbuch zum Neuen Testament* VI (1959), p. 592 especially, see also J. Bonsirven, *Le divorce dans le Nouveau Testament* (Paris, 1948); J. Moingt, "Le divorce 'pour motif d'impudicité,' " *Recherches de Science religieuse* 56 (1968), pp. 337-84 (this article has appeared in German in J. David and F. Schmalz, *Wie unauflöslich ist die Ehe?* (Aschaffenburg, 1969), pp. 178-222, as "Ehescheidung 'auf Grund von Unzucht' "; A. Sand, "Die Unzuchtsklausel in Matt. 5: 31-32 und 19: 3-9," *Münchener Theologische Zeitschrift* 20 (1969), pp. 118-29; F.J. Schierse, "Das Scheidungsverbot Jesu. Zur schriftgemäßen Unauflöslichkeit der Ehe," N. Wetzel, ed., *Die öffentlichen Sünder oder Soll die Kirche Ehe scheiden?* (Mainz, 1970), pp. 13-41; G. Schneider, "Jesu Wort über die Ehescheidung in der Überlieferung des

Neuen Testaments," *TrThZ* 80 (1971), pp. 65–87.

65. An enormous number of books and articles have been written on this theme. Among the most important are B. Kötting, "Digamus," *RAC* 3 (1957), pp. 1016–24; A. Oepke, "Ehe I," *RAC* 4 (1959), pp. 650–66; G. Delling, "Ehescheidung," *RAC* 4 (1959), pp. 707–19; O. Rousseau, "Divorce and Remarriage: East and West," *Concilium* 4 (1967), pp. 57–69; J. Moingt, *Wie auflöslich ist die Ehe?*, op. cit., pp. 178–222; J. Gründel "Ehescheidung im Verlauf der Jahrhunderte," N. Weil et al., *Zum Thema Ehescheidung* (Stuttgart, 1970), pp. 41–60; P. Stockmeier, "Scheidung und Wiederverheiratung in der alten Kirche," *ThQ* 151 (1971), pp. 39–51; H. Crouzel, *L'Eglise primitive face au divorce* (*Théol. hist.*, 13) (Paris, 1971); J. Ratzinger, "Zur Frage nach der Unauflöslichkeit der Ehe," F. Henrich and V. Eid, eds., *Ehe und Ehescheidung*, op. cit., pp. 35–56; P. Nautin, "Divorce et remariage dans la tradition de l'Eglise latine," *Recherches de science religieuse* 62 (1974), pp. 7–24; H. Dombois, *Unscheidbarkeit und Ehescheidung in den Traditionen der Kirche* (*Theol. Ex. heute*, 190) (Munich, 1976).

66. Origen, *In Matthaeum*, 14, 23: *PG* 13, 1244ff.

67. Basil, *Ep.* 217, 77: *PG* 32, 804ff.

68. Ibid., *Ep.* 188, 9: *PG* 32, 677ff; see also *Ep.* 199, 21: *PG* 32, 721.

69. Ambrosiaster, *In Epistulam I ad Cor* 7, 10. 11: *PL* 17, 230.

70. Augustine, *De fide et operibus* 19, 35: *CSEL* 41, 81.

71. The most important synods in this context are those of Elvira (ca. 306), Arles (314), Neocaesarea (314 and 325), Nicaea (325), Laodicea (between 341 and 381) and Carthage (407). See P. Stockmeier, *ThQ* 151 (1971), pp. 45–48; H. Crouzel, *L'Eglise primitive face au divorce*, op. cit., p. 114; H. Dombois, *Unscheidbarkeit und Ehescheidung in den Traditionen der Kirche*, op. cit., pp. 22–28.

72. See P. Manns, "Die Unauflöslichkeit der Ehe im Verständnis der frühmittelalterlichen Bußbücher," N. Wetzel, ed., *Die öffentlichen Sünder*, op. cit., pp. 42–75; P. Mikat, "Zu den Voraussetzungen der Begegnung von fränkischer und kirchlicher

Eheauffassung in Gallien," *Diakonia und ius. Festgabe für H. Flatten* (Munich, Paderborn & Vienna, 1973), pp. 1–26.

73. I have followed the path originally traced out by J. Ratzinger in this interpretation and the conclusions drawn from it. This interpretation has also been confirmed by K. Lehmann in his article "Unauflöslichkeit der Ehe und Pastoral für wiederverheiratete Geschiedene," K. Lehmann, *Gegenwart des Glaubens* (Mainz, 1974), pp. 274–94, especially p. 281ff; and "Nochmals: Wiederverheiratete Geschiedene," op. cit., pp. 295–308 (bibliography).

74. See N. van der Wal, "Secular Law and the Eastern Church's Concept of Marriage," *Concilium* 5 (1970), pp. 76–82; Pierre von Chersonnes (P. L'Huiller), "Ehescheidung in der Theologie und im Kirchenrecht der orthodoxen Kirche," J. David & F. Schmalz, *Wie auflöslich ist die Ehe?*, op. cit., pp. 337–51; O. Rousseau, "Ehe und Ehescheidung in den Ostkirchen," N. Wetzel, ed., *Die öffentlichen Sünder*, op. cit., pp. 94–104; H. Dombois, *Kirche und Eherecht*, op. cit., pp. 197–213.

75. See W. Gloege, "Vom Ethos der Ehescheidung," *Gedenkschrift für Werner Elert*, (Berlin, 1955), p. 356. The Eastern Church's solution to this problem and its theological justification was made known to the bishops of the Western Church during the Second Vatican Council by the interventions of the Melchite Patriarch of Egypt, E. Zoghby; it aroused a great deal of interest. See J.C. Hampe, ed., *Die Autorität der Freiheit* 3 (Munich, 1967), pp. 264–68.

76. See P. Delhaye, "The Development of the Mediaeval Church's Teaching on Marriage," *Concilium* 5, (1970), pp. 83–88; R. Weigand, "Das Scheidungsproblem in der mittelalterlichen Kanonistik," *ThQ* 151 (1971), pp. 52–60.

77. See the *Codex Iuris Canonici*, canon 1128–32. See also U. Mosiek, *Kirchliches Eherecht*, op. cit., pp. 279–92 (bibliography).

78. See the *Codex Iuris Canonici*, canon 1120–24.

79. See the *Codex Iuris Canonici*, canon 1125ff.

80. See the *Codex Iuris Canonici*, canon 1119.

81. See the *Codex Iuris Canonici*, canon 1013, § 2, according to which marriage is essentially indissoluble. With regard to the sacramental nature of Christian marriage, the unity and indissolubility of that marriage have, according to this canon, a "special firmness." For this dynamic statement, see M. Kaiser, "Unauflöslichkeit und 'Auflösung' der Ehe nach kirchlichem Recht," *Diaconia et ius. Festgabe für H. Flatten*, op. cit., pp. 27-43.

82. See Thomas de Vio Caietanus, *Epistolae Pauli et aliorum Apostolorum*, (Paris, 1536), 62 r: In 1 Cor. 7; Ambrosius Catharinus, *Annotationes in commentaria Caietani* (Lyons, 1542), V, 508f.

83. See V.J. Pospishil, *Divorce and Remarriage. Towards a New Catholic Teaching* (London, 1967); W.W. Bassett, ed., *The Bond of Marriage* (Notre Dame & London, 1968); V. Steiniger, *Auflösung unauflöslicher Ehen* (Graz, Vienna & Cologne, 1968), pp. 87-120; P. Huizing, "Unauflöslichkeit der Ehe in der Kirchenordnung," *Concilium* 4 (1968), pp. 582-87, and "Canon Law and Broken Marriages," *Concilium* 7 (1971), pp. 13-21, and "Das katholische Ehescheidungsrecht seit dem Konzil von Trient," N. Wetzel, ed., *Die öffentlichen Sünder*, op. cit., pp. 76-93; A. Gommenginger, "Zur Unauflöslichkeit der Ehe," J. David and F. Schmalz, *Wie unauflöslich ist die Ehe?* op. cit., pp. 77-87; B. Russo, "Die Ehescheidung im Zweiten Vatikanum und in der Rechtstradition der Kirche," *Wie unauflöslich ist die Ehe?* op. cit., pp. 99-161; G. May, "Wie unauflöslich ist die Ehe?" *Archiv für katholis ches Kirchenrecht* 140 (1971), pp. 74-105; H. Herrmann, *Ehe und Recht. Versuch einer kritischen Darstellung* (*Quaestiones disputatae* 58) (Freiburg, Basle & Vienna), 1972, p. 137ff.

84. *DS* 1797-1812; New series, 731-46.

85. *DS* 1327; New series 730.

86. See Martin Luther, *De captivitate Babylonica ecclesiae* (*1520*): *WA* 6, pp. 550-60; *Confessiom Augustana*, XXVIII, *Bekenntnisschriftender evangelisch-lutherischen Kirche*, (Göttingen, ²1952), p. 125; Melanchthon, *Tractatus de potestate*

papae, Bekenntnisschriften, op. cit., p. 494ff.

87. *DS* 1807; New series 741. For the interpretation of this canon, see P. Fransen, "Divorce on the Ground of Adultery—the Council of Trent (1563)," *Concilium* 5 (1970), pp. 89–100. In this article, the author summarized his conclusions made in a whole series of previously published studies (quoted in note 1 of the Concilium article). P. Fransen's interpretation of the teaching of the Council of Trent has been widely recognized as authoritative by many scholars. See, for example, R. Weigand, *Theologische Quartalschrift* 151 (1971), p. 59ff; J. Ratzinger, *Ehe und Ehescheidung*, op. cit., pp. 47–51; K. Lehmann, *Gegenwart des Glaubens*, op. cit., p. 286ff and the bibliography in note 8. More recently, H. Jedin discussed the subject again and in many ways came to the same conclusions in his article "Die Unauflöslichkeit der Ehe nach dem Konzil von Trient," K. Reinhardt and H. Jedin, *Ehe—Sakrament in der Kirche des Herrn*, op. cit., pp. 61–135. In contrast to Fransen, he placed great emphasis on the conciliar claim that its teaching was based on divine revelation. He does, however, demonstrate that the Council only aimed at Protestants, not at the Greeks, some of the Church Fathers, and certain councils. We are in any case bound to question Huizing's minimalistic interpretation in "Das kanonische Ehescheidungsrecht seit dem Konzil von Trient," N. Wetzel, ed., *Die öffentlichen Sünder*, op. cit., p. 79ff, and "La dissolution du mariage depuis le Concile de Trente," *Revue de Droit Canonique* 21 (1971), pp. 127–45.

88. Pastoral Constitution, *Gaudium et Spes*, 4ff.

89. Countless articles and books have been written about this pastoral problem. Full bibliographies will be found in the two contributions by K. Lehmann, op. cit., (see note 73 above) and R. Metz and J. Schlick, *Mariage et divorce* (RIC Supplement 1), (Strasbourg, 1973). Only the most important publications are listed here: J. David & F. Schmalz, eds., *Wie unauflöslich ist die Ehe?* op. cit.; N. Wetzel, ed., *Die öffentlichen Sünder*, op. cit.; H. Heimerl, ed., *Verheiratet und doch nicht verheiratet?* (Vienna, 1970); N. Weil, et al., *Zum Thema Ehescheidung*, op. cit.;

R. Gall, *Fragwürdige Unauflöslichkeit der Ehe?* (Zürich & Würzburg, 1970); the articles in *Concilium* 5 (1970); J. Neumann, "Unauflösliches Eheband? Eine Anfrage zum kanonischen Eherecht," *Theologische Quartalschrift* 151 (1971), pp. 1-22; R. Metz & J. Schlick, eds., *Die Ehe—Band oder Bund* (*Kirche für morgen* 1) (Aschaffenburg, 1971); F. Henrich & V. Eid, eds., *Ehe und Ehescheidung*, op. cit.; W. Löser, "Die Kirche zwischen Gesetz und Widerspruch. Für und wider eine Zulassung wiederverheirateter Geschiedener zu den Sakramenten," *Herderkorrespondenz* 26 (1972), pp. 243-48; J. Fuchs, *Die Unauflöslichkeit der Ehe in Diskussion* (K. Rahner & O. Semmelroth, *Theologische Akademie* 9) (Frankfurt a.M., 1972), pp. 85-107; H. Lubsczyk et al., *Ehe lösbar?* (Berlin, 1972); the articles in *Recherches de science religieuse* 61 (1973), pp. 487-624; the articles in *Concilium* 7 (1973); K. Hörmann, *Kirche und zweite Ehe. Um die Zulassung wiederverheirateter Geschiedener zu den Sakramenten* (Innsbruck, 1973); P. Huizing, ed., *Für eine neue kirchliche Eheordnung. Ein Alternativentwurf* (Düsseldorf, 1975).

90. See *Codex Iuris Canonici*, canon 1138-41.

91. See *Codex Iuris Canonici*, canon 1119.

92. See U. Mosiek, *Kirchliches Eherecht*, op. cit., p. 70ff.

93. Thomas Aquinas, Suppl. 49, 3 ad 7.

94. See H. Rahner, "Der Schiffbruch und die Planke des Heils," *Symbole der Kirche. Die Ekklesiologie der Väter* (Salzburg, 1964), pp. 432-72.

95. See D. Bonhoeffer, *Ethik* (Ethics) (Munich, 1966), pp. 124-27 (justification and scarring).

96. For a discussion of this question, see H.B. Meyer, "Können wiederverheiratete Geschiedene zu den Sakramenten zugelassen werden?," J. David and F. Schmalz, eds., *Wie unauflöslich ist die Ehe?* op. cit., pp. 269-306; H. Heimerl, "Sakramentenempfang für Wiederverheiratete," *Theologische Quartalschrift* 151 (1971), pp. 61-65; H. Socha, "Kirchenrechtliche Überlegungen zum Kommunionempfang ungültig Verheiratete," *TrThZ* 81 (1972), pp. 298-309; K. Hörmann, "Kirche und zweite Ehe"; W. Löser,

"Die Kirche zwischen Gesetz und Widerspruch," *Herderkor-respondenz* 26 (1972), pp. 243-48; K. Lehmann, *Gegenwart des Glaubens*, op, cit., pp. 276-79; U. Mosiek, *Kirchliches Eherecht*, op. cit., pp. 76ff (bibliography); J.B. Hirschmann, *Die Zulassung wiederverheirateter Geschiedener zu den Sakramenten (Theologische Akademie* 12) (Frankfurt a.M., 1975), pp. 104-15; H. Heinemann, "Die Teilnahme wiederverheirateter Geschiedener an der eucharistischen Tischgemeinschaft als Frage an das kanonische Recht," *Theologie und Glaube* 66 (1966), pp. 161-77; A. Zirkel, *Schließt das Kirchenrecht alle wiederverheirateten Geschiedenen von den Sakramenten aus?* (Mainz, 1977). An outline of the arguments for and against will be found in the resolution passed by the German Synod of Bishops: "Christlich gelebte Ehe and Familie," 3. 5. 2.

97. A. Zirkel's work, *Schließt das Kirchenrecht alle wiederverheirateten Geschiedenen von den Sakramenten aus?*, unfortunately only came to my attention when my own book was with the printer. If Zirkel's interpretation of canon law, namely that not all those who have divorced and remarried are necessarily excluded from the sacraments, is correct, then my dogmatic attempt to find a solution to the problem may be in accordance with canon law as it is at present. To quote Zirkel's words, "Not to admit many of those who have divorced and remarried to the sacraments, but to exclude everyone would mean that the current law of the Church would have to be changed. Not a change in that law, but its application would in many cases open the way for many such people to receive the sacraments" (p. 54).

98. The definition of marriage in Roman law is as follows: *coniunctio maris et feminae et consortium omnis vitae, divini et humani iuris communicatio* (Dig. 32, 2, I, 21; quoted in Leclercq and David, *Die Familie*, op. cit., p. 31 and H. Dombois, *Unscheidbarkeit und Ehescheidung*, op. cit., p. 91). This definition and its all-embracing view also determined the theological tradition. See Peter Lombard, *Sent.* IV, 27, 2; Thomas Aquinas, Suppl. 44, 3; *Roman Catechism*, II, 8, 3.

99. For this problem, see P.J. Huizing, "Kirchliche und

standesamtliche Trauung," *Liturgisches Jahrbuch* 22 (1972), pp.
137–47, and "Canon Law and Broken Marriages," *Concilium* 7
(1973), pp. 13–21; K. Richter, "The Liturgical Celebration of
Marriage. Problems Raised by Changing Theological and Legal
Views of Marriage," *Concilium* 7 (1973), pp. 72–87; U. Mosiek,
Kirchliches Eherecht, op. cit., pp. 70–80 (bibliography).

100. See the summary in the article on marriage and family life
("Ehe und Familie") in *StL* II (⁶1958), p. 1001ff.

101. See Pius VI, *Const. Auctorem fidei* (1794), condemning
the statements made by the Council of Pistoia: *DS* 2658–2660;
Pius IX, *Syllabus* (1864): *DS* 2966, 2973; see also 2991; Leo XIII,
encyclical *Arcanum divinae sapientiae*: *DS* 3145; Pius XI, encyclical *Casti connubii*: *DS* 3713.

102. See *Codex Iuris Canonici*, canon 1012 § 2.

103. See the summary in Leclercq & David, *Die Familie*, op.
cit., p. 38ff; see also the article "Ehe und Familie," *StL* II (⁶1958),
pp. 995ff, 1016ff.

104. See the Pastoral Constitution *Gaudium et Spes*, 36, 60.

105. See Thomas Aquinas, Suppl., 49, 3 ad 7.

106. Although the conditions are different, this is similar to the
two levels in the contract of marriage that existed in Germanic
law, in which a distinction was made between betrothal as a contract between clans and marriage as acceptance into the community. See the summary of this law in H. Dombois, *Unscheidbarkeit und Ehescheidung in den Traditionen der Kirche*, op.
cit., pp. 19ff, 84ff, etc.; see also the article "Ehe und Familie,"
StL II (⁶1958),p. 1000ff.

107. See *Codex Iuris Canonici*, canon 1016.

108. See *Codex Iuris Canonici*, canon 1138ff.

109. See *Codex Iuris Canonici*, canon 1075.

110. See the resolution in the text of the German Synod of
Bishops, *Christlich gelebte Ehe und Familie*. 4. 1. 2.

111. See the Dogmatic Constitution on the Church, *Lumen
Gentium*, 16.

112. It is usual to speak of the *intentio faciendi quod facit ecclesia*; see *DS* 794, 1262, 1313, 1611.

113. See the various manuals of dogmatic theology, such as F. Diekamp and K. Jüssen, *Katholische Dogmatik nach den Grundsätzen des heiligen Thomas*, 3 (Münster, [11]1954), p. 390; the article on "Intention II," *Lexikon für Theologie und Kirche* V ([2]1960), pp. 723ff.

114. Thomas Aquinas, *Summa theologiae* III, 64, 9 ad 1: *Non obstante infidelitate (minister) potest intendere facere quod facit ecclesia, licet aestimet id nihil esse. Et talis intentio sufficit ad sacramentum.*